Uyghur Women Activists in the Diaspora

Bloomsbury Studies in Religion, Gender, and Sexuality

Series Editors: Dawn Llewellyn, Sonya Sharma and Sîan Hawthorne

This interdisciplinary series explores the intersections of religions, genders, and sexualities. It promotes the dynamic connections between gender and sexuality across a diverse range of religious and spiritual lives, cultures, histories, and geographical locations, as well as contemporary discourses around secularism and non-religion. The series publishes cutting-edge research that considers religious experiences, communities, institutions, and discourses in global and transnational contexts, and examines the fluid and intersecting features of identity and social positioning.

Using theoretical and methodological approaches from inter/transdisciplinary perspectives, *Bloomsbury Studies in Religion, Gender, and Sexuality* addresses the neglect of religious studies perspectives in gender, queer, and feminist studies. It offers a space where gender can critically engage with religion, and for exploring questions of intersectionality, particularly with respect to critical race, disability, post-colonial and decolonial theories.

Becoming Queer and Religious in Malaysia and Singapore,
Sharon A. Bong
Beyond Religion in India and Pakistan,
Navtej K. Purewal and Virinder S. Kalra
Experience, Identity & Epistemic Injustice within Ireland's Magdalene Laundries,
Kathrine van den Bogert
Narrative, Identity and Ethics in Postcolonial Kenya,
Eleanor Tiplady Higgs
Street Football, Gender, and Muslim Youth in the Netherlands,
Kathrine van den Bogert
Women and the Anglican Church Congress 1861–1938,
Sue Anderson-Faithful and Catherine Holloway

Uyghur Women Activists in the Diaspora

Restorying a Genocide

Susan J. Palmer, Dilmurat Mahmut, and
Abdulmuqtedir Udun

BLOOMSBURY ACADEMIC
LONDON • NEW YORK • OXFORD • NEW DELHI • SYDNEY

BLOOMSBURY ACADEMIC
Bloomsbury Publishing Plc, 50 Bedford Square, London, WC1B 3DP, UK
Bloomsbury Publishing Inc, 1359 Broadway, New York, NY 10018, USA
Bloomsbury Publishing Ireland, 29 Earlsfort Terrace, Dublin 2, D02 AY28, Ireland

BLOOMSBURY, BLOOMSBURY ACADEMIC and the Diana logo are trademarks of Bloomsbury
Publishing Plc

First published in Great Britain 2024
Paperback edition published 2026

Cover design: Rebecca Heselton
Cover image © Kuzzat Altay TBC

A catalogue record for this book is available from the British Library.

Library of Congress Cataloging-in-Publication Data
Names: Dilimulati, Maihemuti, editor. | Udun, Abdulmuqtedir, editor. |
Palmer, Susan J., editor.
Title: Uyghur women activists in the diaspora : restorying a genocide /
Susan J. Palmer, Dilmurat Mahmut, and Abdulmuqtedir Udun.
Description: 1st. | New York : Bloomsbury Academic, 2024. |
Series: Bloomsbury studies in religion, gender, and sexuality |
Includes bibliographical references and index.
Identifiers: LCCN 2023038073 (print) | LCCN 2023038074 (ebook) |
ISBN 9781350418332 (hardback) | ISBN 9781350418370 (paperback) |
ISBN 9781350418349 (pdf) | ISBN 9781350418356 (epub)
Subjects: LCSH: Women–China–Xinjiang Uygur Zizhiqu–Social conditions. |
Minority women–China–Xinjiang Uygur Zizhiqu–Social conditions. | Women,
Uighur–Biography. | Women, Uighur–Political activity. | Uighur
(Turkic people)–Crimes against–China. | Genocide–China–Xinjiang Uygur Zizhiqu.
Classification: LCC HQ1769.X565 U94 2024 (print) | LCC HQ1769.X565 (ebook) |
DDC 305.40951/6–dc23/eng/20231011
LC record available at https://lccn.loc.gov/2023038073
LC ebook record available at https://lccn.loc.gov/2023038074

ISBN: HB: 978-1-3504-1833-2
         PB: 978-1-3504-1837-0
         ePDF: 978-1-3504-1834-9
         eBook: 978-1-3504-1835-6

Series: Bloomsbury Studies in Religion, Gender, and Sexuality

Typeset by Integra Software Services Pvt. Ltd.

For product safety related questions contact productsafety@bloomsbury.com.

To find out more about our authors and books visit www.bloomsbury.com
and sign up for our newsletters.

Contents

Figures

Note on the Authors

Susan J. Palmer is a researcher and writer in the field of new religious studies. She is an Affiliate Professor and Lecturer in the Religions and Cultures Department at Concordia University, and a Lecturer at McGill University's School of Religious Studies, both in Montreal, Quebec. She has written several sociological studies of new religions, notably, *Moon Sisters, Krishna Mothers, Rajneesh Lovers: Women's Roles in New Religions* (1994); *Aliens Adored: Rael's UFO Religion* (2004); *The New Heretics of France* (2011); *The Nuwaubian Nation: Black Spirituality and State Control* (2010), and (with Stuart Wright) *Storming Zion: Government Raids on Religions* (2015).

Dilmurat Mahmut obtained his Ph.D. in Educational Studies from McGill University. Currently, he is a FRQSC postdoctoral fellow at Concordia University, and a course lecturer at McGill University, Canada. His research interests include Muslim identity, education, violent extremism, and immigrant/refugee integration in the West. His publications appeared in various academic journals such as *Diaspora, Indigenous and Minority Education, Journal of Muslim Minority Affairs, Taboo: The Journal of Culture and Education, Journal for Deradicalization, Forum for International Research in Education, Journal of the Council for Research on Religion*, and *Identities: Global Studies in Culture and Power*. He has also authored and co-authored multiple book chapters.

Abdulmuqtedir Udun is a Uyghur researcher and a rights advocate based in Ottawa, Canada. After arriving in Canada in 2018, Udun has worked and volunteered for several Uyghur organizations as an editor, interpreter and researcher contributing to raising awareness on China's genocide of the Uyghurs. He worked as a research assistant at the School of Religious Studies, McGill University on the SSHRC-funded project "Children in Sectarian Religions and State Control" for two years from October 2020 to September 2022. He speaks fluent Arabic and English.

Acknowledgments

We would like to express our gratitude to Professor Gerbern Oegema, founder and Chief Editor of *The Journal of the Council for Research on Religion* (JCREOR) at McGill University for his kind encouragement and support of our conferences and research efforts. We owe a special thanks to Amanda Rosini and Elyse MacLeod, both JCREOR editors, for their critiques of earlier versions of this work and for sharing with us their sophisticated grasp of the emerging field of narrative analysis. We thank the Social Sciences and the Humanities Research Council of Canada for supporting our research. We thank our fellow researchers, Marie-Ève Melanson, Shane Dussault Ovadia, Sean Remz, Maryam Amirdust and Sarah Boyer who contributed so much during the early phase of our Uyghur project. Finally, we must express our gratitude to all the Uyghurs we have worked with, Mehmut Tohti and Kayum Masimov of the Uyghur Rights Advocacy Project in Ottawa, and of course to the brilliant and courageous Uyghur women who consented to be interviewed.

Introduction

This book explores the life stories of ten women Uyghurs living in the diaspora who are prominent in the international Uyghur advocacy movement. Born in the 1970s or early 1980s in East Turkestan/Xinjiang, each woman chose to leave China and live in the West. Today, settled in North America, the United Kingdom or France, some of them have academic or professional degrees and hold official positions in Campaign for Uyghurs, the World Uyghur Congress, or other major human rights NGOs.[i] One is a professional journalist with Radio Free Asia. Two are camp survivors who have spoken out before the United Nations and the Uyghur Tribunal. All these women are striving to raise public awareness of the Chinese government's ongoing campaign against the Uyghurs, Mongolians, Tibetans, Hui, Kazakhs, and other Turkic peoples of Asia Minor.[ii]

Since January 2021, there have been signs of progress.[iii] The United States, under Trump's administration, recognized the PRC's crimes against humanity as a "genocide." Secretary of State Mike Pompeo issued a public statement: "I believe this genocide is ongoing, and that we are witnessing the systematic attempt to destroy Uighurs by the Chinese party-state [who has] engaged in the forced assimilation and eventual erasure of a vulnerable ethnic and religious minority group." In February 2021, Canada's House of Commons voted 266 to 0 to declare China's treatment of its Uyghur minority population as a genocide.[iv] Since then, seven other countries have also formally recognized China's persecution of the Uyghurs in Xinjiang as a "genocide."[v] The United Nations human rights office,[vi] and France's National Assembly, in a March 2022 resolution, accused China of perpetrating "crimes against humanity."[vii] Similar resolutions have been reached by parliamentary bodies in the United Kingdom, the Czech Republic,[viii] Belgium, the Netherlands, France, Lithuania, and Ireland.[ix] Most recently, on December 27, 2022, the Taiwanese parliament or "Legislative Yuan" officially recognized that the Chinese government has been committing genocide and "crimes against humanity" targeting the Uyghur people.[x] Nuri Turkel, in his 2022 book, *No Escape*, offers a useful account of the history of human rights sanctions against China and the complex process different countries faced as they debated whether China's treatment of the Uyghurs qualified as a "genocide" under the Geneva Convention. He also notes that the phrase, "crimes against humanity" lacks the "sheer power that the word 'genocide' holds in the collective imagination."[xi]

The Research Project

In February 2020 the four members of our research team at McGill University began to interview Uyghurs in the diaspora.[xii]

It was in the early days of the COVID-19 pandemic when most people had lost their employment or abandoned their workspace and were staying and working from home. Uyghur men and women, some of them refugees, others landed immigrants, skilled laborers, or students with visas, were taking online courses in English and French, or learning new job-related skills on the internet. Many were immersed in remote lessons on the Qur'an (a forbidden activity in China). We interviewed these people (referred to by the McGill Research Ethics Board as our "human subjects," our "informants" or "research participants")[xiii] on Zoom or Skype.[xiv] Often their children played in the background or climbed upon their laps, since schools and daycares were closed. Sometimes the wife or daughter would translate for the man of the household. The two Uyghur members of our team, Dilmurat and Abdulmuqtedir, functioned as interpreters and "worldview translators," providing political and cultural commentary during the interviews.

Over two years we interviewed thirty-eight Uyghurs; twenty-one who lived in Canada, seven in Turkey, and ten of the most prominent women Uyghur advocates and activists[xv] who were living in Canada, the U.S., France, Australia, or the U.K.

The research started in February 2020 with our visit to the new Uyghur School set up in Chateauguay, a small village just outside Montreal, Quebec. Organized by parents, the aim was to instruct their children in the Uyghur language and culture. Our SSHRC-funded research project was called, "Children in sectarian religions and state control" and we were interested in writing an article on the school, since we had read about the mass sterilizations of Uyghur women in China and the forcible apprehension of Uyghur "orphans" who were placed in high security boarding schools and indoctrinated in CCP values, forced to eat pork, and forbidden to speak Uyghur or retain any elements of their native culture. Since our research focused on the state's intrusion into the family life of minority religions, Uyghur schools in the diaspora seemed to be a promising topic.

After we observed the Uyghur language class and watched the children sing and dance, we spoke with the parents who ran the school. We were struck by their dramatic stories about why they left China and decided to interview more Uyghurs. Word spread that a group of researchers from McGill University were studying their community. Our sample snowballed as our interviewees suggested we contact their friends. Other Uyghurs contacted us after hearing about our study from a WhatsApp group for Canadian Uyghurs. We decided to conduct a survey, "The Uyghurs in the Diaspora in Canada." Our aim was to gather information on the Uyghurs who left their Homeland (East Turkestan/ Xinjiang) and relocated to Canada. The survey consisted of forty-five questions on why and how these immigrants came to Canada and what challenges they faced in China. Our respondents numbered 106, and our findings indicate that they were subject to widespread discrimination and oppression in China before emigrating to Canada. Other questions explore their contact with relatives in their Homeland and their level of religiosity since arriving in Canada. Other questions focused on how they were attempting to preserve their Uyghur culture and language while living in diaspora. Our survey was published in 2021 in the *Journal of the Council for Research on Religion*.[xvi]

This research presented unique ethical issues. Many of our "informants" feared the "long arm" of China if they spoke out, citing incidents of "enforced disappearances" of Uyghur critics in China, Egypt, and Kazakhstan.[xvii] They expressed their fear that if they participated in our research their relatives still living in the Homeland (East Turkestan) would be punished. Despite these concerns, we noted in our Uyghur "informants" an eagerness, even a strong determination, to speak up about injustice and atrocities their people face in China.

These people fit what Canada's research ethics boards would deem as "vulnerable human subjects"—and yet, considering their unique and dire plight, it seemed unethical *not* to encourage them to speak up. During the research process we took the standard precautions of using fake (Uyghur) names and avoided identifying data such as naming the city they lived in.[xviii] We required our participants to sign consent forms and we stored the interviews in external drives.

Our research team at McGill University interviewed these ten women activists via Zoom or Skype at the height of the COVID-19 pandemic, between 2020 and 2022. The interviews were conducted in English, French, or the Uyghur language. Our subjects spoke about growing up in Uyghur-speaking households, where prayer and Qur'an study had to be performed in secret. They spoke of leaving their home province, East Turkestan/Xinjiang, to study in Mainland China's top universities where, as ethnic Uyghurs, they encountered systemic racism and historical revisionism. As young women, most of them graduated with top marks and high expectations of finding a "dream job," hoping to launch meaningful careers—only to discover that, as non-Han Chinese, they were ineligible for employment in most companies and teaching colleges, especially in their own Homeland. Several women personally witnessed the terrifying events surrounding the February 1997 Ghulja Incident (a.k.a Ghulja Massacre) and the 2009 Urumqi riots, where hundreds of young protesters were gunned down by police during peaceful demonstrations and thousands more were arrested arbitrarily and sent to prisons. Each woman identifies her "personal tipping point" (or "turning point") when she faced the realization that, "I could no longer live in my own country."[xix]

What is unique and significant about these life stories is that they provide Western audiences with vivid glimpses of what life must have been like for Uyghurs *before* the contours of a genocidal campaign against the Turkic people of the XUAR region became visible in 2017 when it was broadcast through the international media. The first detailed reports of ongoing atrocities inside Xinjiang's "re-education camps" appeared in the *New York Times*, the *Guardian*, and *Washington Post* in 2017—the same year that Uyghurs living abroad experienced a complete shut down of all communication with family and friends in China. When our research subjects chose to emigrate from China, it was in the late 1980s. 1990s or early 2000s, and they had no idea that a "campaign of genocide" was being put into place. In hindsight, however, they realize what they personally experienced (what had prompted them to leave) were the early warning signs of a vast, well-coordinated "social engineering project"[xx] that entailed the suppression of Uyghur language, culture, religion, and personal freedom. By leaving China, these women avoided the cataclysmic period that soon followed; a period of the arbitrary arrests, extrajudicial prison sentences, forced indoctrination and torture, the implementation of high-tech surveillance, and a ruthless process of ethnic segregation and denigration.

In this study we adopt a narrative analysis approach to these women's life stories. We consider them as a form of oral history which eloquently communicates the harsh experiences of ethnic Uyghurs living in China in the 1970s to the early 2000s during the CCP's ongoing crackdowns and "Strike Hard" campaigns. Relying on the techniques of narrative analysis, our team investigates and analyzes the tensions, turning points, and motivations which led to our subjects' personal transformations, prompting their decisions to become publicly involved in creating social and political change.

While the political statements of most of these women—Zubayra Shamseden, Rushan Abbas, Rahima Mahmut, Rukiye Turdush, and Dilnur Reyhan, in particular—have been widely circulated in the British, French, Canadian, Australian, and U.S. media and quoted in government reports—their personal stories have not previously been made available to the public.[xxi] When we conducted the interviews, rather than eliciting their political views, we chose rather to focus on their family backgrounds in the Uyghur communities of East Turkestan, on their academic careers in Chinese universities, and on the troubling, traumatic events in their teens and twenties which triggered their decisions to leave China. It is our conviction that by making these narratives public, they might bolster their political activities by adding depth and social context to the unfolding story of a genocide.

Part One

Personal Narratives as an Extension of Uyghur Advocacy Work

Our interest in the Uyghurs began in February 2020, when three members of our research team visited the Uyghur language school in Châteauguay, a village near Montreal, Quebec. As a minority religion in China that is heavily controlled by the state, the Uyghurs appeared to be relevant to our research project.[i]

The school was set up by a group of Uyghur parents for the purpose of teaching their children the basics of Uyghur language and culture. Later, we realized what an important and urgent task this was, given the Chinese Communist Party's (CCP) recent campaign to erase the Uyghur culture and orphanize the Uyghur children. After incarcerating their parents in "re-education camps," many of the children are placed in boarding schools where they are indoctrinated in CCP ideology and forbidden to retain any elements of their cultural heritage or to converse in their native language.[ii]

Our initial aim was to study Uyghurs in the diaspora, with a special focus on how they were raising their children in Canada. However, when we spoke with the parents at the school, we quickly realized that their main interest was in sharing their bitter experiences of discrimination and persecution in their "Homeland,"[iii] and explaining to us why they chose to leave China. Given our interest in engaging with this community, we followed their lead, and broadened the scope of our research to include their personal narratives of life in China. While several Uyghurs we approached declined to participate in our research, due to security concerns (fearing the CCP would retaliate against their relatives in China), we easily made new contacts through our initial inquiries, and we ultimately developed a cordial relationship with ten of the pre-eminent female Uyghur leaders in the international diaspora, all fully engaged in their mission to alert the West to the ongoing atrocities occurring in China's "re-education" camps.

These women did not share the school parents' security concerns. Unlike tens of thousands of Uyghurs in the diaspora who prefer to keep a low public profile for fear of reprisals against their relatives in the Homeland, these women have gone public. In their common vocation to become the "Voice of the Uyghurs," they are willing to be interviewed, named, and photographed.

Since the Chinese Communist Party's "Strike Hard" campaign against Uyghurs in 2014, it has become increasingly difficult—and since 2017 virtually impossible—for Uyghurs to emigrate from China.[iv] Like most Uyghurs living in the diaspora, our women activists arrived well before this campaign was initiated, and we were interested in hearing why they had chosen to emigrate, and what events or influences had shaped their decisions to embrace a new career of political advocacy. Their anecdotes, which eloquently describe their personal trajectories towards political engagement, provide an important window into the everyday discrimination and low-level persecution that was ongoing before the PRC's campaign of genocide was fully implemented and became visible to the West.

We call these personal histories a "restorying" because they pose a bold challenge to the historical and political framing of the Uyghurs' situation in Xinjiang that is currently proffered by Chinese ambassadors and news outlets controlled by the CCP.[v] Accordingly, we opted to use an interview method informed by oral history, as the oral history interview is both "a powerful technique" for qualitative researchers looking to capture the lived experience of a person or particular group of people, as well as a well-recognized resource for social justice, insofar as "testimony as oral history becomes a way to move toward social justice."[vi] In line with the acknowledgment by contemporary scholars that the oral history interview yields a narrative of lived experience rather than a strictly factual account of the past, we conclude this study with a narrative analysis of these women's life stories.

Narrative Analysis and Methodology

Oral history should be understood as more than just a subfield of history. As David King Dunaway describes it, oral history is "a *method* (oral data collection), a *subfield of history* (oral historiography), and a *resource* for teachers, communities, and researchers of all kinds (oral history)."[vii] As these distinctions suggest, the method of oral history is transdisciplinary, and what the oral history interview yields is not merely a resource for the historiographer. While earlier iterations of oral history tended to be uncritical, presenting oral history interviews as transparent transmissions of "the truth" of past events based on eye-witness accounts, contemporary approaches to oral history are much more critically self-reflexive. They acknowledge and even emphasize, "the profound role of memory, language, culture and interaction when recounting past events."[viii]

Many contemporary researchers understand the oral history interview in narrative terms, as a speech exchange that unfolds in a specific "situational and interactional context," which aims to "elicit *storytelling*, often for an imagined audience."[ix] While the story being told is intended to be "a comprehensible account of the past,"[x] as noted above, not all researchers utilizing the method of oral history are interested in framing or analyzing the data they collect in historiographical terms. Indeed, as Dunaway notes, researchers from a variety of fields in the social sciences and humanities view these "accounts of the past" as personal and/or cultural *stories*, which, accordingly, can be analyzed from the framework of narrative analysis.[xi]

This approach to oral history acknowledges that "individual memory is often fallible and [...] routinely influenced by [one's] social environment,"[xii] while simultaneously maintaining that the narratives provided are, nevertheless, valuable resources. By probing "the *construction* of the stories people tell when asked to talk about themselves and their communities,"[xiii] we gain important insight into the lived experience of the narrator(s) as well as the wider historical, cultural, and socio-political network of relations they find themselves embedded in. As Martin Cortazzi puts it, narrative analysis can therefore be understood as "opening a window into the mind, or, if we are analyzing narratives of a specific group of tellers, as opening a window on their culture."[xiv] As these comments on oral history interviews indicate, there are three broad considerations that must be accounted for when analyzing oral history interviews in narrative terms: (1) narrative construction; (2) narrative space and time, (3) imagined/intended audience.[xv]

The first consideration, narrative construction, is wide-ranging, and seeks to answer questions such as: Is the narrative told in a linear or non-linear fashion? What terminology is employed by the teller—or tellers—when describing their experiences? Is their narrative structured to make, or to emphasize, a particular point? Is there a break between the beliefs of the storyteller(s) and how things actually were? How do the narrative constructions of multiple tellers compare? Are there similarities or differences? The second consideration, narrative time and space, attempts to account for the specific temporal and spatial context in which the interview takes place, and how this context influences the way the narrative takes shape. The final consideration, imagined/intended audience, acknowledges that every narrative is told with a purpose which informs how the teller(s) construct their narrative, which details they choose to include/ omit, how they describe and characterize events, places, people, and so on. In our study, we draw from the growing body of oral history/narrative discourse which identifies storytelling as a resource for social justice,[xvi] and ultimately argue that these women's narratives are best understood as a continuation of their activism.[xvii]

The Research Method and Terminology

The interviews were conducted on Zoom or Skype, primarily in English, but also in French (with Marie-Ève's help) and in the Uyghur language (interpreted by Dilmurat and Abdulmuqtedir). In several interviews we switched between languages. The interviews were recorded, but Palmer wrote notes by hand during the interviews. After our team listened to the recording, some parts were transcribed, and the notes and transcriptions were re-read several times to identify patterns and themes in the narrative, which we then analyzed in light of the three considerations outlined above (narrative construction, narrative space and time, and imagined/intended audience).

We conceptualized our interviews as "a type of guided conversation."[xviii] This is to say, we gave our subjects the opportunity to recount their stories with minimal prompting or attempts to steer them in specific directions. We did compose an interview schedule, but we were flexible in responding to our subjects' lead. We tried to stick to open-ended questions while actively listening, and to pose follow-up questions, as needed, to invite our subjects to deepen and expand the story being told.[xix]

Ollerenshaw and Cresswell advise researchers to collaborate with their participants in such a way as to narrow the gap between the narrative told and the narrative reported, so that the participant has an active role in the restorying process.[xx] In our McGill University-administered research project, Palmer, Mahmut, and Udun tried to facilitate this process. First, we insisted our participants sign a consent form. Second, we sent them a copy of the transcript of their interview, inviting feedback. Third, during the final process, we invited our participants to respond to our edits and interpretations of their stories. Several of them added additional anecdotes or corrected our information, or challenged our interpretation of their story. In this way, they enriched their narratives and "owned" their personal narratives more completely. This suggests that restorying allows synergy between the data gathering and analytical processes within research.

An important note on terminology relates to how we have decided to refer to the Uyghur "Homeland." Naming the Uyghur's native land is a highly politicized issue. While the "Turkic-speaking migrants from Mongolia from whom the present-day Uyghurs claim descent" have been present in the Tarim Basin region—now the Southern part of Xinjiang—since the first millennium BCE, various Chinese dynasties have sought, with varying degrees of success, to control this region since the first century of the current era, when "the Han dynasty (206 BC–AD 221) military campaigns of Bao Chao [first] brought the Tarim Basin [...] under Chinese control."[xxi] However, "genuine Chinese control over its northwestern frontiers, rather than political influence or a tributary relationship" was only achieved by the Qing dynasty in the eighteenth century, and the Xinjiang region (a name which translates to "New Frontier") "was only formally incorporated into the Chinese empire as a province in 1884."[xxii] In the early twentieth century, Uyghurs and other Turkic peoples—who had never fully left the region despite ongoing Chinese expansionism—began to formally resist Chinese control.[xxiii] These efforts first bore fruit on November 12, 1933, when the First East Turkestan Republic was established in Khotan. The Republic was short-lived, lasting only until February 6, 1934, "when Kashghar was taken by the forces of Ma Zhongying."[xxiv] However, the end of the First Republic in 1934 did not put an end to Uyghur opposition to Chinese control, and in 1937 another resistance effort was launched, resulting in the establishment of the second East Turkestan Republic in 1944, which lasted until 1949.[xxv]

Given this history of contention over the Uyghur-populated region, by calling it "East Turkestan," one is siding with the oppressed natives or Uyghur "nationalists," and by calling it "Xinjiang," one is siding with the colonizing Han Chinese. Accordingly, we will proceed with the dual term, "East Turkestan/Xinjiang," to acknowledge this politicized tension.

Why Women?

We should explain at the outset why we have chosen to focus exclusively on female activists. After all, there are many outstanding male activists in the Uyghur diaspora, notably Dolkun Isa, a former student-leader of the pro-democracy demonstrations at Xinjiang University in 1988. Isa fled China in 1994 and is now President of the Munich-based World Uyghur Congress.[xxvi]

Nuri Turkel is another outstanding example. He was the first Uyghur in the U.S. to earn a law degree and he is now part of the United States Commission on International Religious Freedom (USCIRF). Although he states in his 2022 autobiography, *No Escape*, that he is a lawyer, not an "activist," his book and his interviews in the media have been very effective in raising public awareness of the ongoing genocide in East Turkestan/Xinjiang.[xxvii]

But we have chosen to focus on Uyghur women for three reasons.

First, we must consider women's role within Uyghur culture. According to Bellér-Hann, in traditional Uyghur households, Uyghur women were primarily responsible for childcare, cooking, cleaning, and other household chores before 1949.[xxviii] In a similar vein, Mahmut and Smith Finley, in their study of "gendered" Uyghur proverbs reveal that the number of proverbs highlighting men's role in national politics and the importance of male over female accounted for more than a third of a total of seventy-two male-related proverbs. Conversely, the proverbs emphasizing feminine obedience, subservience, and the central role of women in domestic life comprised more than a third of 164 proverbs gathered from five collections of Uyghur proverbs published in Xinjiang. The authors also spotted three proverbs specifically depicting women's political apathy.[xxix] Thus, it appears reasonable to assume that the process of carving out a career in political activism in the Uyghur diaspora has been a greater, more radical leap into public life for women than it has been for men.

However, despite the overt discouragement of women's involvement in national politics in the traditional Uyghur culture, one finds the presence of several heroines in Uyghur literature. Among such examples is Nuzugum (1808–30) who has become a symbol of Uyghur resistance to Manchu colonialism and stands out "as a trope of nationalism."[xxx] In the original narration by Molla Bilal binni Molla Yusup in 1882 (and many others have rewritten his account of the story since), Nuzugum, a young Uyghur woman from Kashgar, kills a Manchu official she is forced to marry. Her story lives on, constantly retold in public and private gatherings of Uyghurs. As Abramson (2012) points out, "the resiliency of the story's gendered themes underscores the role of gender as an influence on contemporary Uyghur political advocacy and a defining component of communal consciousness."[xxxi] Even so, the fact is that examples of Uyghur heroines are rare, compared to the wealth of examples of Uyghur heroes; Uyghur women rarely appear as political leaders in Uyghur history or literature.

But this situation has changed during the final decades of the twentieth century. Uyghur women, especially university graduates, appear to have emancipated themselves from traditional gender roles to a great extent, as a direct result of the global feminist movement. Our participants, who grew up in that era, reflect this situation in the lived experiences they have shared with us.

While Smith Finley claims in her 2015 study that Uyghur women working in the hospitality sector (bars, hotels, restaurants) have faced the contempt of Uyghur men, which has led to conjugal and religious tensions,[xxxii] it should be noted that the hospitality sector does not represent all public workspaces. It is well known that contemporary Uyghur women are working in government offices, educational institutions, the healthcare system, businesses, and other sectors. They have pursued careers in these fields where they are endorsed and supported by Uyghur men.

Our interviews with Uyghur women activists reflect this new status quo. Some of their mothers were professionals; Rushan Abbas' mother was a doctor, and Gulchehra Hoja's mother was a professor of pharmacology. Both Rushan Abbas and Arzu Gul had supportive fathers who encouraged them to excel in school and succeed in the job market.

Yet, since 1949 the Chinese Communist state has not tolerated any signs of political agency in the Uyghur population, either from men or women. In its campaigns it has aimed to further depoliticize Uyghur women as obedient civilians who are "good at the singing and dancing"; this stereotypical rhetoric has become especially salient in the more recent era of anti-religious extremism.[xxxiii] Since 2017, such rhetoric has become even more political, forcefully promoting Chinese songs that praise the Chinese Communist Party, while erasing all religious elements from the Uyghurs' daily life and soundscapes.[xxxiv] Paradoxically, the Chinese government aims to "liberate Uyghur women from oppression" by forcing them to remove their hijabs and replace their modest clothing with a "modern" dress code.[xxxv]

The Chinese government has specifically targeted conspicuously successful academic, professional, and religious Uyghur women. Viewed by their fellow Uyghurs as shining examples of culture and identity, these women were arrested on trumped up or obscure charges and sent to prison or simply "disappeared."[xxxvi]

Rebiya Kadeer is a heroine among Uyghurs, an extraordinary business entrepreneur, millionairess, and political activist. She recounts her tale of persecution in *Dragon Fighter*.[xxxvii] Born in China's Altai Mountains where her father was a gold miner, she married at 15 and helped support her six children by selling handmade clothing on the black market. Divorced by age 28, Rebiya Kadeer remarried to a Uyghur intellectual and dissident, Sidik Rouzi, and launched various trading operations throughout Central Asia. By 1993 she was the wealthiest woman in China. Kadeer was patronized by the

Chinese Communist Party as a successful Uyghur, and in 1995 Rebiya Kadeer served as a delegate to the United Nations Conference on Women in Beijing.

Kadeer capitalized on her business ventures to employ and mentor Uyghurs. She promoted education in the Uyghur language and opened foreign-language schools in Kashgar, Hotan, and Aksu. She funded a political campaign to aid the Uyghur population and spoke out about Uyghur human rights issues and hardships in Xinjiang. Her political activities led to her arrest in August 1999, and in March 2000 she was tried and convicted of endangering national security by furnishing state intelligence abroad. During her five-year imprisonment, she won the 2004 Rafto Prize for Human Rights by Norway and was nominated for the 2006 Nobel Prize for Peace.

Since her release from prison, Rebiya Kadeer has lived in the U.S. where she continues to campaign for Uyghur human rights.

Another striking example of how the CCP silences distinguished Uyghur women leaders is Dr. Rahile Dawut, a renowned anthropologist who specialized in Uyghur Islamic *mazars* (shrines). She disappeared into the re-education camps in late 2017.[xxxviii]

Rahile Dawut, born in Kashgar in 1966, was one of the first Uyghur women to earn a Ph.D. at Beijing Normal University. In 2007 she founded the Ethnic Minorities Folklore Research Center at Xinjiang University. She had always avoided politics and was a staunch member of the CCP, but on December 12, 2017, Rahile Dawut disappeared at Urumchi where she was scheduled to fly to Beijing for a conference. Later, in July 2021, the Chinese authorities confirmed that she was sentenced to prison, without offering details. In 2020, Rahile Dawut became the first Open Society University Network's Honorary Professor in the Humanities. "Rahile Dawut is internationally recognized as a leading authority on Uyghur cultural life and practices," said Leon Botstein, OSUN Chancellor. "She has trained a generation of young scholars in the study of the region's folklore and tradition, and her rigorous and illuminating work has become a portal through which the global community has been able to discover the richness of Uyghur culture."[xxxix]

In 2016 during the new Xinjiang Party Secretary Chen Quanguo's crackdown on religious books, Dawut noticed that her books were disappearing from bookstores and library shelves.

Since her mother's disappearance, Akida Pulat, who is a university student in the U.S., has become an activist, using social media as her platform. In 2020 Rahile Dawut was the recipient of the Scholars at Risk "Courage to Think" award. Akida Pulat, received the award on her mother's behalf and made the following speech:

> My mother is a scholar, not a criminal. She studies the folklore and cultural traditions of minority populations … She has been doing research within the strict confinement of censorship imposed by the Chinese government. What makes my mother's eyes sparkle are the ancient sites, the deserts and villages and the folk customs that have stood the test of time.[xl]

Our research participants are all professional women who do not fit into women's domestic role in Uyghur traditional culture, as discussed at the beginning of this section. Here we need to emphasize that these ten women are not "typical" Uyghur women; they are the ones who received higher education, or who excelled in business (like Zumrat Dawat), or who rose to the top of their profession (like Gulchehra Hoja). They have transcended Uyghur traditional gender norms and have defied the Chinese government's expectations of them. They are a minority among a minority.

Having said that, our interviews suggest many of our subjects' parents do not fit neatly into Uyghur traditional gender roles. Rushan Abbas's mother was a doctor, and Gulchehra Hoja's mother was a pharmacist and professor of pharmacology (i.e., not confined to the domestic role). Both Rushan Abbas and Arzu Gul had supportive fathers who encouraged their daughters to excel in school and prepare for a professional career.

It is also possible that the women who received their secondary education in Chinese schools and/or universities might have been influenced by the Chinese post-Maoist unisex culture. After the Chinese Communist Revolution in 1949, dramatic measures were enacted to promote social equality between men and women. The famous quote from Mao Zedong (*c.* 1968) reflects the commitment of the emerging People's Republic of China: "Women hold up half the sky." Since emigrating to Western countries, these women have encountered Western feminist ideas and social milieux.[xli] Thus, a more nuanced analysis is required.

Kabir Qurban, a young Uyghur activist from Surrey, British Columbia, declared in our March 2020 interview that women are more numerous than men in advocacy groups and accomplish most of the work. But somehow, he noted, men get most of the credit:

> I've talked to Palestinian activists, Yemeni activists, Syrian activists, there are more women in this field than men. When you look at the actual people within

the organizations, there are more women ... The presidents, vice-president ... they will be the guys, but the women do the work, they are the ones organizing events, booking the venues, connecting to different allies, writing the articles. And men are the ones that shake hands, hand over the prizes.

Qurban also suggested that women are better equipped temperamentally for advocacy work. Men, who are preoccupied with their role as breadwinner for the family, tend to repress their emotions, whereas "women are more troubled by the genocide than the men."[xlii]

Women are more emotionally driven ... it really hits them hard. I am an emotional dude, I write poetry. I talk to many Uyghur guys [about the genocide], they feel it, but when I say the same thing to a Uyghur girl, she will break down in tears, whereas a Uyghur guy, he will be like 'wow, that's tough.' I guess women have more emotional capacity ... they are driven to the cause much faster. Men, we do what we can, but at the end of the day, we are not as emotional.

Mihrigul Tursun also suggested that women are more effective in advocacy work than men:

We do more than men, I think. Women are emotional, they don't think too much, they make decisions quickly when they want to do something. Men think too much before doing something.[xliii]

The second reason we focused on women activists is their testimonies have shaped the international media's harrowing descriptions of detainees' lives inside what the Chinese government proudly refers to as its "re-education camps" (what the Uyghurs routinely refer to as "concentration camps"). While the number of men arrested and incarcerated in these camps probably exceeds the number of women, and the very first victim to speak out in 2017 (as a witness of camp atrocities) was a Kazakh man, Omir Bekali,[xliv] it has been, overwhelmingly, the female camp victims whose testimonies are broadcast through media reports and published in biographies.

Kabir Qurban observed how journalists seem to prefer interviewing women: "They do, look at which Uyghur survivors are prominent: Tursunay Ziyawudun, Mihrigul Tursun—but you don't see as many articles about Omir Bekali [but he also] suffered quite traumatically, right?"

One might argue that journalists prefer female victims because they are more "newsworthy." Rahima Mahmut declared in her interview on Radio Free Asia that Uyghur women have been the most effective source of firsthand information about the internment camps:

It is primarily these brave women of ours who have spoken about the terrifying things inside [the camps]. They have spurred discussion in the world by speaking in detail about intensely private things, things that people are normally too afraid to speak about. There has been a great power in this.

Rahima Mahmut interviewed the rape victims for BBC News,[xlv] and she points out that it is the female survivors who offer firsthand accounts of the violent prison culture of systemic rape and other crimes perpetrated on Uyghur and other Turkic women in the camps. (It seems reasonable to assume that men are less likely to disclose rape experiences.)

Zumretay Arkin, a young Uyghur woman who works with the World Uyghur Congress in Munich, Germany, claims that "the Chinese government is using women to facilitate this genocide."

Uyghur women are one of the main targets … If you look at … the survivors who managed to flee, who are sharing their stories, most of them are women. It is this kind of incredible resilience and strength that women have. Despite enduring the most egregious crimes such as sexual violence, they are still the ones voicing out their concerns with the international community. Just imagine how much strength that takes! Many men don't have that strength. For me, it shows how women in our country are extremely resilient, they are powerhouses. They were the ones exposing this genocide; without them the international community wouldn't be as aware. In our culture, men are not used to sharing personal experiences and details.[xlvi]

Uyghur Women and the Mass Sterilization Program

Several of our women activists have insisted that the Chinese government's mission to reduce the Uyghur population in Xinjiang has largely been implemented by targeting women's reproductive faculties; through forced sterilizations, medication, and injections to reduce fertility, IUDs, and mandatory abortions. Nury Turkel, in *No Escape*, includes a chapter on "The War on Uyghur Women," in which he asks how "messing with women's bodies" could possibly be a tactic to control "terrorists"?[xlvii] German anthropologist, Adrian Zenz, also raises this question in his article, "Sterilizations, IUDs and Mandatory Birth Control."[xlviii]

An article that appeared in ANI, South Asia's Multimedia News Agency, echoes the arguments of Nuri Turkel and Adrian Zenz, pointing out that

"Uyghur women have found themselves the targets of some of Beijing's cruellest tactics meant to slash birthrates which have dropped 24% in 2019 in Xinjiang, compared to 4.2 nationwide. But women have also been the fiercest fighters for Uyghur freedom and self-empowerment." The ANI refers to Asiye Abdulahed, "a Uyghur woman who in 2019 leaked the first trove of secret files that documented the camps' existence." This move unleashed a flood of threats against her and her family and made her a heroine among Uyghur activists.[xlix]

The Beautification and Sinocization of Uyghur Women

Timothy Grose, in his 2019 article, tracks the CCP's recent efforts to transform the appearance of Uyghur women and to "discipline their bodies."[l]

Grose notes that in 2011, "Chinese officials unrolled *Project Beauty*, a five-year, $8 million dollar multi-media initiative that encouraged piously-dressed Uyghur women to 'look towards "modern" culture' by removing face veils and jilbāb." By 2015, new legislation had outlawed hijab, *lichäk*, as well as "abnormally long" beards and clothing featuring the star and cresent moon symbol in public areas. In 2017, the CCP introduced the "Three News" campaign, a package of study sessions and workshops to "advocate a new lifestyle, establish a new atmosphere, and construct a new order." Timothy Grose points out that, "buried beneath the campaign's jargon is the 'prohibition against wearing strange clothing.'" Although the language is ambiguous, he finds it "signals the CCP's recommitment to standardizing and sinocizing sartorial practices among Uyghurs, especially women."

Grose concludes: "Officials confidently predict that this campaign will transform Uyghur women into docile Chinese subjects." As a representative from the XUAR's Women's Federation explained, "the Beauty Parlor and Hair Salon initiative will bring forth three transformations in the lives of women. First, women will transform their body image. Then, they will transform their way of life. Finally, they will transform their way of thinking."[li]

The Emergence of Uyghur Feminism?

The third reason we chose to study Uyghur women is that we discerned a unique strain of feminism in their statements. When they explained their rationales for getting involved in political activities, they tended to view their role in "gendered" terms, often referring to themselves as "mothers" trying to protect their people as their "children." Rebiya Kadeer, the very first outstanding Uyghur woman activist, declares in her book: "I want to be the mother of the Uyghurs, the medicine for their sufferings, the cloth to wipe their tears, and the shelter to protect them from the rain."[lii]

Many of our female subjects have embraced a maternal, protective role, self-identifying as the "Voice" of all the Uyghurs who have been detained, who have "been disappeared" in the genocide. As Mihrigul Tursun explained in our interview:

> I love my family, but I don't just think just about [them], I have to think about all the Uyghur people. I have to become the *voice* of the Uyghurs. If everyone keeps quiet, then the whole Uyghur people will be gone. I have to become the voice of those who are in the concentration camps, and all those who died in them.[liii]

Zumrat Dawut has also vowed to be the voice of her silenced loved ones:

> People like my mother, my sisters, my brother, they remain hopelessly in those camps without any fault. They do not have a voice. They cannot tell the world what is happening. They cannot speak even though they are innocent. So now I have the chance, and I choose to be their voice.

The Concept of Japakesh

In the traditional culture of Uyghur Muslims, there is a concept called *japakesh* which is applied to exemplary women. The Uyghur word *japa* means "suffering, difficulty, burden, or toil." The suffix, *kesh*, turns the noun into an adjective that depicts a person who bears a heavy burden while facing many challenges. Thus, *japakesh* denotes "the moral character of those who are hard working and persevere despite obstacles, who put others' benefits before their own."[liv] The ideal Uyghur woman is *japakesh*, meaning she is selfless, long-suffering, carrying a heavy burden, and deferring her own pleasure, comfort, and well-being for the sake of her family. Being called *japakesh* is high praise. As Cindy Huang (2009) notes, *a japakesh* person is the one who "perseveres through difficulty, suffers with a moral purpose. In conversation on matters big and small, Uyghur women [consider it] as both praise for one's hard work and empathic recognition of one's troubles."[lv]

We found that Uyghur women activists are recasting, reinterpreting the traditional ethic of *japakesh*, in a manner not unlike what Rosemary Ruether discovered in her study of women in the Christian Social Gospel movement in nineteenth-century America. She discerned a new, emerging Christian strain of feminism, which she calls, "Reformist Romantic feminism."[lvi]

Ruether proposes three types of feminisms in the history of Christian thought: *Eschatological, Liberal,* and *Romantic.* Unlike the other two types, *Romantic* feminism emphasizes the differences between male and female as representative of complementary opposites. Under the category of "Romantic Feminism," Ruether identifies four subtypes. Her third subtype, "Reformist Romanticism" retains the notion found in "Conservative Romanticism" of Woman as pure, as eschewing sin, and as wife and mother confined to the domestic sphere. But for the "Reformist Romantic feminist, the bourgeois ideal of the family is seen as a convenient launching pad for a wider mission into the world, in order to uplift and transform society to higher standards of justice and peace." Ruether writes, "Women's mission [was] to uplift ... male institutions to the higher standards of the home ... Women, as educators of children, must become founders of schools ... As the keepers of cleanliness, they should [fight] against dirt and disorder, ranging from physical dirt to political corruption. [Their motto was] 'a new broom sweeps clean.'"

Ruether explores how conservative domestic images of woman in nineteenth-century America were reconfigured in the Christian Social Gospel crusade of political reform to propel women into a new dynamic role, so they could "clean up City Hall." We have found, in the course of our interviews, that women involved in the Uyghur advocacy movement are expressing a new, emerging strain of feminism informed by their Turkic Islamic culture, which involves a redefinition of *japakesh.*

Zubayra Shamseden explains how she reconstructed her identity as a Uyghur woman:

> In the almost 30 years since I've left my home, I have revised my idea of what a Uighur heroine should be. The role of heroine should no longer be only for the woman of sacrifice, the "burden-bearer" who exemplifies the moral strength of *japakesh.* Instead, our most admirable Uighur women should be those who simply forge ahead to achieve greatness.[lvii]

Ruether writes,

> In its most visionary moment, reformist romanticism glimpses the contours of a new society characterized not only by honesty, purity, and cleanliness, but above all by peace. The nature of woman in incompatible with war ... reformists don't think women can accomplish this by staying a home ... Women must

enter the workplace and use their higher instinct to change its social structures and relationships. They must have *power*. They need the vote and the right to education and to political office.

This passage could be referring to contemporary Uyghur women activists, whose work involves confronting a hideous war on their people. Their "glimpses of a new society" would be their common vision of regaining East Turkestan for the Uyghur people, of expelling the Han settlers and Beijing's puppet politicians. They envision rebuilding the minarets, legalizing the *Qur'an* and prayer mats, reviving the *meshreps*, and opening travel to Mecca. They imagine bringing back women's headscarves, men's beards and *doppas*. But first, they must liberate the incarcerated Turkic prisoners from "re-education" facilities, tear down the check points, and turn off the surveillance systems. Then they will build new cemeteries and hold memorial services in the mosques for the dead. With this vision in mind, they have each pursued a path to education and established a social position, a "power spot," that allows them to engage in Uyghur advocacy.

Here it would be worthwhile to reflect upon our discussion on pathways from feminine docility to positions of power, and how it appears to conflict with some of our participants' aspiration to restore the traditional Islamic way of life in their Homeland. At first glance, their re-embracing of Islam resembles the piety movement among Egyptian Muslim women who are forging a new type of Islamic feminism, according to Saba Mahmood's analysis.[lviii] However, we would argue that these Uyghur women's desire to revive Uyghur Islam has been primarily triggered by China's assault on Uyghur religious identity. Their renewed passion for Islam is an essential component of the future task of restoring and promoting a liberal Homeland culture. This ambition appears to have prompted some of them to privately revisit their own religious identity more seriously—a process that is revealed in the narratives of some interviewees, such as Zubayra Shamseden, who shares her thoughts about hijab and her piety. It is interesting to note that, unlike the Iranian women, who held death-defying demonstrations against wearing the hijab in late 2022, for Uyghur women, the hijab has become a symbol of freedom, of personal liberation, and empowerment.

Part Two

The Narratives

In what follows, our participants narrate the series of events in their personal lives that informed their decisions to leave China and influenced their separate paths towards becoming public advocates for the Uyghur cause.

The ten Uyghur women we interviewed for this project are Zubayra Shamseden, Rushan Abbas, Rahima Mahmut, Rukiye Turdush, Arzu Gul, Raziya Mahmut, Dilnur Reyhan, Gulchehra Hoja, Zumrat Dawut, and Mihrigul Tursun. The first six women are human rights activists working with various human rights groups and are involved with the international Uyghur Advocacy movement. Dilnur Reyhan is an academic living in Paris who is frequently interviewed by the French media. Gulchehra Hoja is a journalist and author who works for Radio Free Asia. She explained to us that she objects to being identified as an "activist" because in her career (journalism), it is important to maintain her objectivity and avoid expressing personal opinions in public. Nevertheless, the information she gathers and disseminates is invaluable for the Uyghur cause. Moreover, her story about why she left China is an important one because it sheds light on the Chinese government's plan to assimilate Uyghur children. The last two, Zumrat Dawut and Mihrigul Tursun are both survivors of the infamous "re-education" camps who have chosen to share their experiences of torture and other atrocities before the United Nations, the Uyghur Tribunal, and with international news outlets. Thus, they are first and foremost "whistleblowers." However, they are also "activists" because they participate in demonstrations, work with Uyghur advocacy groups, and they continue to speak out against the ongoing violations of human rights in China.

Each narrator refers to her personal experiences and to historical events that occurred in China between the 1970s and the early 2000s. We have enriched each narrative with endnotes, some of which provide resources for further reading on the issues/events being discussed, others which offer factual corrections (names, dates of events, etc.) or supplementary commentary. It is important to note that, although these women have significant public profiles due to their advocacy work, the narratives recounted here have not, at this time of writing, been told publicly. Two exceptions are found in the "whistleblowers," Zumrat Dawut and Mihrigul Tursun, whose survivor stories have been broadcast in the media, in biographies co-authored with journalists, and even in cartoons.[i] Even so, guided by our questions, their narratives in this book contain new stories and more detail on their personal lives.

1. Zubayra Shamseden

Interviewed on February 18, 2021

Zubayra Shamseden was born in Ghulja city[ii] (also known as Yining city) in East Turkestan (which China calls "the Xinjiang Uyghur Autonomous Region"). She emigrated to Australia in 1993 after marrying an (Uyghur) Australian, and later immigrated to the United States in 2009. For over thirty years she has defended the

Figure 1 Zubayra Shamseden. Photographer: Munawwar Abdulla.

human rights of Uyghurs and other Turkic people in East Turkistan, working for academic and government nonprofit organizations. Her work involves outreach, translation, research, and administration for the Uyghur community. She has a certificate in Chinese from the Industrial University of Xinjiang; a B.A. in Library and Information Science from East China Normal University, Shanghai; a diploma in Russian language and literature from the State University of Eastern Kazakhstan; and an M.A. in International Studies from the University of South Australia. She is fluent in Uyghur, Chinese, Uzbek, English, and Russian. Zubayra Shamseden is the Vice President for the World Uyghur Congress. She also works as Chinese Outreach Coordinator for the Uyghur Human Rights Project in Washington, D.C., networking with pro-democracy Chinese groups, Hong Kongers, Taiwanese, and other Chinese-speaking communities. She has three children and lives in Virginia, USA with her husband, who is also a Uyghur activist.[iii]

Childhood and Family

Zubayra Shamseden was born and raised in Ghulja city of East Turkistan, growing up in a religious and intellectual family. Her grandfather Munawwar Emin was a landlord and imam; he was persecuted by Chinese authorities from 1950s, lived under house arrest until he passed away in 1984. Her father, Shamseden Munawwar, was also an imam. He gave clandestine lessons on Islam for children and adults in the family home, in the early morning or late at night, so as to avoid notice by the authorities. Zubayra recalls how she and her siblings, "were very little, and we thought these people [who came to our home] were people in need and our parents were helping them. But we didn't know they were teaching them religion." Zubayra's parents also secretly instructed her in Islam. They told her not to tell anyone about family prayers, or the visitors who came at dawn or dusk. She grew up realizing her family had always engaged in "some kind of secret resistance towards the Chinese Communist regime":

> One of my uncles was imprisoned, and my grandfather spent most of his life under house arrest because of the Chinese Communist regime; but my parents didn't tell us anything because they were too afraid to talk about what's happening to us and why it's happening.

Growing up in Ghulja, Zubayra sensed vaguely that "something was wrong." At her Chinese school, she recalls how "people of my background" used to face regular discrimination. Her grandfather put a bold spin on this as "a sign from God." "Grandfather used to say [about the discrimination we Uyghurs faced in school]: 'You know, that's maybe God's help; God has saved you from becoming a communist!'"

Studies in China

Zubayra left Ghulja when she was 16 to study at the East China Normal University in Shanghai. There she completed her B.A. in Library and Information Science. During her studies, she took part in a protest in Shanghai in support of the Tiananmen protest.

> At the time, we were young, and we thought that through knowledge, communication and hard work we would be able to improve the situation of our people's lives. And that was my ambition.

During her student career in Shanghai, Zubayra became aware of how Han Chinese and Uyghurs were treated differently. This became clear as soon as she arrived at her girls' dormitory of the university:

> When I arrived my room in the dormitory, I found six Chinese girls who were staring at me: "Oh, what are you doing here? You should go back to the foreigners' dormitory!" they said. (The school had foreign students who came from other countries, so they thought I mistakenly got into their room when I should be in a different building.) I told them: "No, I'm not a foreigner, I'm also from China." And they said: "We don't have people like you living in China." And then I said: "I'm from Xinjiang." One of them replied, "Are you saying you are from Xinjiang or from Singapore?" I said, "No, Xinjiang. Do you know Xinjiang?" Very few knew. One of them said: "Oh yes, Xinjiang, there are a lot of horses and wild people." It was just like, "wild people riding horses all day, illiterate, backward bunch of people … is that the place that you come from?" So I said, "Yes."

> It was such an interesting stereotype! Kind of ignorant. I was very surprised to see that people in one of the top universities, top students, educated in foreign languages with very good grades … they had so little knowledge about China. I told them: "In high school, we keep learning that Xinjiang was part of China since ancient times, that we belong to China, but you don't seem to know that. What kind of things did you learn in high school?"

> That was my question. And they said: "The Great China." "And did you ever learn about Uyghurs? Where we are? How our land looks like?" They had no idea. All they knew was … horses … backward bunch of kebab sellers. But after a while, many of them kind of realized that things were completely different than they thought. Even that we were more educated than them. Because I told them, I told them all our history.

Free Speech in Shanghai *versus* Xinjiang

Zubayra observed that there was much more freedom of speech and opportunity to engage in intellectual debate in Shanghai than in East Turkestan:

> At least when you talked about that kind of stuff you didn't get arrested, or asked to go to the police office, or forced to do political studies to "educate your mind." In Shanghai you are free to talk. And I was free to talk to my roommates, free to talk to my lecturers, anybody. And, you know, many of them kind of liked it, especially those Chinese who had never been to East Turkestan and never learned properly about us. Many of them were really interested and wanted to learn. I even became close friends with many of the Chinese students too. And later, especially after the Tiananmen Square massacre, many Chinese students said to me: "You should be independent." I remember some were saying: "You should be able to lead your own country. This is China, and China just killed its own people. If war happens, they're going to kill you first." That's what my Chinese friends would say at the time because they were free to talk.

Zubayra graduated in 1990 and was offered a good job in Shanghai, but she turned it down because she wanted to go back to East Turkestan to put her knowledge at the service of her people:

> Although the Chinese government keeps saying that East Turkestan has been part of China since ancient times, in many ways, the two places [mainland China and East Turkestan] are completely different—especially in terms of freedom and the treatment of people. From the time of my student life [in Shanghai], I felt like, whatever was okay to do in Shanghai should be okay to do in East Turkestan as well. And that's why my ambition … I was offered a job in Shanghai, but I refused. I said: "Look, what we say here in Shanghai; that the people in East Turkestan are behind, that the region is behind, underdeveloped … well, it would be possible to be as developed as the rest of China if we received equal treatment. But the Uyghurs are not treated as equal to the Han Chinese people. So, as a graduate, I'm going back to East Turkestan and that's what I'm going to do." (That was the mind that I had at the time.)

Returning to East Turkestan in the 1990s

Zubayra found a job in Urumqi, the Capital city of East Turkestan, at the Academy of Science, which was considered at the time to be an excellent opportunity. As she explains, the only reason she was hired was because her Chinese professor recommended her, and her "first foreign language" at the university happened to be Russian. There was a high demand for Russian speakers at that time.

On arriving, her first task was to introduce the computer to the Academy of Science. There were only two computers in the whole Academy and while waiting for the new ones to arrive, Zubayra worked as a translator. She explains that "in the Chinese system, they often hire you for one thing, but then you end up doing whatever they ask you to do. So, instead of working with computers I ended up doing only Chinese–Russian translations."

When asked if she had faced discrimination as a woman working at the Academy of Science, Zubayra replied there was always some form of discrimination against women, including Chinese women: "Being a Uyghur is hard but being a Uyghur woman is even harder." She told the story of how she supported the candidacy of a young Uyghur woman at the Academy of Science who, in the end, was not selected. The hiring team had expressed their concern that this woman candidate might get married and have children, so then she might ask for some time off.

Zubayra was shocked by this attitude, but when she questioned the committee's decision, she got into trouble. "The situation is worse for Uyghur women," she observed, "because they are identified as Muslim and therefore seen as more family-oriented."

After six months of working at the Academy of Science, she began to notice the repression of Uyghur intellectuals, in terms of promotions, publishing, and opportunities to direct or publicize research projects. ("Han Chinese would go first, then Uyghurs were second in East Turkestan.") Zubayra was assured by her employers that Uyghur intellectuals received unequal treatment simply because they were not fluent in Chinese, "but I knew plenty of Uyghur intellectuals at the Academy who were fluent, not only in Chinese, but also in Russian, English, and Japanese."

> So, this kind of unequal treatment really hurt me. In Shanghai, in this kind of situation, they would have chosen the ones that were the most qualified, most knowledgeable. But it didn't happen for Uyghurs. And from that time, I started to question: "You say that we are a part of China from the ancient times, and yes, we've been ruled by one party which is the Chinese Communist Party, and we've been ruled by Beijing—so why is there such a different treatment? Is it geographical—that we are Xinjiang and they are Shanghai … is that's how it works?"

But when she asked her employer these questions, she was advised she could only access a good position if she stopped asking questions. Zubayra notes, "I began to think my future was not at the Academy of Science and tried to figure out how I could leave the country."

In the early 1990s the Chinese government was encouraging its citizens to study abroad. America was the most popular destination, then other Western countries and finally, Russia. After six months of working at the Academy, Zubayra registered for a Russian exam that would allow her to study in Russia. The Academy of Science congratulated her on passing the exam and appeared to regard her favorably, since they needed a Russian speaker to continue doing business with Russia. She was sent to study to the U.S.S.R. (today Kazakhstan) in the year 1991–92. During her stay, in December 1991, Kazakhstan gained its independence from Russia. When she returned to Urumqi, she was required to give a report to the Academy:

> At the first staff meeting after I was back, I said: "It was a great experience. After one month that I was there, the country got its independence. The freedom was just a fantastic thing because everyone was enjoying it and that feeling affected every student where I was studying."

> But just that one thing I said began the trouble. After that, I was constantly questioned, "Why did you say this?" ... Every week, the Academy of Science authorities—the political section—would question me. At first, it was them, then it was the Party Secretary who said to me, "because of the Party's great kindness, and because of the Communist Party's greatness, you were able to go to Russia and now you are so knowledgeable in Russian." But the main thing they wanted to know was always, "What did you *do* in Russia?"

I said, "Look, you sent me to Russia to study Russian, what do you think I did?" And they would say, "Look, we know that now, many separatist movements are going on in Central Asia, and you told us that after one month that you were in Russia, Kazakhstan got independence. The word 'independence' is a very sensitive word. Why would you bring it up at the meeting?"

> And I said that I didn't know there was going to be independence when I was there, and when I came back I had to report, so I did it at the first staff meeting ... Then they just began to ask: "Do you have this kind of mind about independence?" I said, "Yes, I know the Kazakhs got independence, what is wrong with that? Yes, Russia is completely fallen down. Not only Kazakhs got independence, Uzbeks got independence, Tajiks got independence ... Yes,

everyone is independent, so what is wrong with that? Yes, we are China, we are independent too, that's just the same thing"

But they said: "No no no! There is something behind what you say!" [*laughs*] 'Those kind of paranoid, stupid questions! And at that time, I didn't have this kind of deep mind of what will happen in the future, but that really affected me. I thought: 'So, what did I do wrong? Why do I have to waste time with you instead of focusing on my work, my job at the Academy, why do I have to waste my time like this?"

Zubayra explains that one of the difficulties for Uyghurs working in a scientific organization in China is that the people who make the decisions are rarely other scholars or researchers. They are loyal members of the Communist Party who have "no idea about what you do." Zubayra notes, "they are often quite illiterate. Some do not even have a high school degree, and they get their high-ranking jobs through connections, by constantly repeating political slogans, and by strictly applying the Party line."

In 1993, a close Uyghur colleague at the Academy of Science who spoke fluent Japanese suddenly disappeared for one month. When he reappeared, "he was very quiet and behaved like a propaganda machine." Later, Zubayra heard that he had been detained and tortured for that missing month. He had been offered a job in Japan, but the Academy had refused to let him go. When he tried to argue against the Academy's decision, he had been detained, tortured and subjected to "political education."

When she realized what had happened to him, Zubayra became frightened. She secretly went to see her old Chinese professor who was knowledgeable about Chinese politics. She complained to him about how she was constantly questioned simply because she had traveled to Kazakhstan.

This professor was very old and less afraid to speak, so he warned me in an explicit fashion that my ethnicity could get me into trouble. Among Uyghurs, everyone kind of speaks in code, implying things rather than stating them clearly. But this professor, he was very explicit, and it confirmed my decision to leave.

Emigrating to Australia

Zubayra was a professional translator with a diplomatic passport. She also had a fiancé in Australia. She requested that her diplomatic passport be exchanged for a standard one, and her fiancé sent her a letter of invitation to visit him in Australia.

When she explained her situation to the Australian Embassy, they told her to get a visa and do a health check—and that was it. She soon left for Australia.

She was surprised at how easy the process was. Her fiancé, a Uyghur, was an Australian citizen, having arrived there as a "White Russian" refugee with his family in the late 1970s. In 1993, her fiancé came to East Turkestan, they got married, and then he returned to Australia. She explains that, from the outside, it looked like she left China *because* she got married, but in fact she had decided it was the best way to leave without putting her family members in trouble. She hadn't told any of her relatives that she was being questioned every week, and if she married an Australian, no one would suspect that she had left China for political reasons.

But when she told the Academy of Science she was leaving, they insisted that she reimburse all the salary she had received until then. They threatened to report her to Border Security if she didn't pay every single *yuan* she had earned in full before leaving. It was the equivalent of two to three years of salary (around 7,000 yuan). She feared if she did not comply, she would be stopped at the airport. She also hoped to return to East Turkestan one day, so she felt she had no other option but to pay.[iv]

After Zubayra had settled down with her husband in Adelaide, she enrolled in graduate studies in Information Studies and found employment at the university. Then she switched to International Relations and was hired by her university to work as a researcher.

Experiencing the Ghulja Massacre from Abroad

Zubayra explains that her decision to study International Relations was motivated by the terrible events in Ghulja in 1997:

> My life changed once again in 1997 because of the Ghulja massacre that happened in my hometown [while I was in Australia]. And that completely changed me. I decided to completely change my profession. So that's when I decided to study International Relations—because I didn't know how I could help my people— starting with my whole family. So, I did further studies and community activities [in Australia]. I started a Uyghur language school, which I managed for over 10 years, until I came to America. So, my life completely changed. I completely devoted myself to this cause.

She learned about the Ghulja Massacre over a phone call to her sister while Zubayra's parents were visiting her in Australia. Chinese technology was not so highly developed at the time, in terms of spyware, so they were able to communicate safely. Her sister had gone into labor on that fateful day when the Ghulja protest started, and her brother-in-law described over the phone how they had been driving through the city on their way to the hospital, but they were constantly blocked because there were so many protesters on the street. He described them as, "normal, unarmed citizens with nothing in their hands," and reported to Zubayra what they had witnessed. Zubayra concludes:

> I can say that we witnessed a horror! I also had an afterwards report. They arrested my brother, they shot my cousin, and one of my nephews got killed. You know, they were only 24 and 23 years old. My sister and my niece were arrested. It just became a war zone. That completely changed my life … It was then that I started to advocate and tell people what was happening. Also, after 1997 a lot of people were resettling. So, I did some work with the United Nations to help Uyghurs resettle in other countries. I was directly involved with the whole process with Amnesty International and the United Nations.

Zubayra is convinced that the Ghulja protest might never have taken place if the government had focused properly on handling the drug [heroin] and alcohol problems in the XUAR region. Instead, she believes that the government deliberately created and fostered this problem.

> Many families were troubled and having a really hard time because someone in the family was using drugs and was spending the family's money on drugs. The drug problems could have been solved if the authorities had made an effort to stop the drug peddlars, or if they had offered young people jobs or created opportunities for their future—but no efforts were made. Instead, the police seemed to be concerned with arresting young, healthy male Uyghurs for no valid reasons.

Zubayra explained that the drugs the young people were taking at the time was a new problem; that, historically, the Uyghurs were not drug users, and it appeared that the heroin trade had been deliberately introduced in East Turkestan through Mainland China, so it was a problem that the Chinese government had the power to stop.

> And because the government did not want to take care of the problem and arrest the drug sellers, young Uyghurs took it upon themselves to resolve the situation by organizing these big *meshreps*.[v] The Chinese authorities did not like it. They accused them of conducting terrorist activities and stopped them.

> The purpose [of organizing a big soccer game] was just to have a match. Uyghurs love soccer so much. Uyghur boys have great skills. So that's one of the things

that can mobilize a lot of people, it can make young Uyghur people concentrate on something meaningful [instead of drugs]. And that was one of the aims.

She explains how the Uyghur *meshrep* leaders had organized a big soccer match in August 1995. They had booked the Ghulja stadium with the authorities, but then the authorities did everything they could to stop the match. They flooded the stadium with water that froze overnight and put big granite stones in the middle of the stadium. When the three soccer managers (who were also the *meshrep* leaders) tried to argue against the decision, they were arrested and sent to prison. Many of the young men in training for the match were targeted by the police who suspected they were engaged in terrorist training.[vi]

Political Engagement

In 2021, Zubayra was elected as Vice President of the World Uyghur Congress for the 2021–24 term. Zubayra's current title at the Uyghur Human Rights Project (UHRP) is Chinese Outreach Coordinator. Her job is to reach out to Chinese speakers around the world in the Chinese language and to educate them about the Uyghurs:

> I mostly reach out to Chinese speakers and educate them about the Uyghurs in the Chinese language. Because many Chinese people, they don't understand what is happening to Uyghur people. Many think that the Uyghurs are very ignorant, but in reality, the Chinese government has a huge propaganda machine … They do the worst [indoctrination] on the Chinese people to get them to back the authorities' decisions to crack down on the Uyghur people. So, to me, it's very important to change the beliefs of the Chinese on what's really going on from a Uyghur perspective … Many Chinese people will say that the Uyghurs are bad people; a bad, unsatisfied minority that has been offered so many privileges, so many incentives, and such support from the Chinese authorities, but are never satisfied. Unsatisfied, unhappy, illiterate, backward Uyghurs who only know how to serve kebabs. And Xinjiang—East Turkestan—is just a kind of lost land, an empty rural land that needs to be developed, so the Chinese need to resettle there. So, that's the kind of education that they get from the Chinese propaganda machine … And when they learn about us, they realize that this is again one more secret that the Chinese government hides from its own people. That's why I think it's very important for us to educate Chinese people, especially ordinary Chinese people.

Zubayra notes that UHRP reached out to Chinese speakers by translating all the documentation they had into Chinese and distributing them on social media. She attends any event she was invited to where there are Chinese people, including meetings with the Taiwanese, Hong Kong, or Chinese Human Rights groups. She found that even groups advocating for human rights in China were reluctant to work with UHRP at first, because they were uncomfortable with the idea of independence. But little by little, she managed to convince them that the Uyghurs should be included in their discussions, that the Uyghurs' claims were legitimate.

> When we would say "East Turkestan" instead of "Xinjiang," they were scared at the beginning. They would say, "It's separatism." And we started to educate them. We said: "Look, it has nothing to do with separatism. East Turkestan *is* our Homeland. This is history. This is our lives. And we are Turkic people, not Chinese. Turkestan means 'the land of Turks,' or 'the land of Uyghurs,' that's how simple it is. And it's just East of Turkestan, which already exists, this is history." That's how we start to educate them. And the thought is also that we just want to be free, you know? We tell them: "We've been ruled with deception by the Chinese government, you know that. They have given us a so-called 'autonomous region,' but we don't have autonomy. If we had autonomy, what is happening today [to Uyghurs in their Homeland] would not be happening. So that's the problem, that's the issue." [As far as] Lay, ordinary Chinese people, we understand. It's ok, they don't know about it, that haven't heard about it. But [to the] knowledgeable Chinese people who wish for a democratic China where everyone has rights and freedom to express themselves ... we say, "you should understand how we feel. That's how *you* feel. You are outside of China, and you fled from your country because you didn't like your regime. Imagine what that regime can do to us. The regime that oppressed *you*? It's the same ... but even more oppressive towards us. That's the problem. We have a lot in common. If you want to get rid of this oppressive regime, we should work together."

> And that's what we've been pledging and calling for. That's how I started to educate. And, gladly, there are a lot of Chinese intellectuals and lawyers and they started to understand what we were talking about ... So now we have a lot of support from Chinese groups, and they now deliver our message to their audience. So that's how we have started to expand.

Zubayra Shamseden explained that her ultimate (if challenging) goal is to have visibility in China. She opened a Chinese social media account to disseminate the information, but it was labeled as "separatist" by the authorities and eventually closed down.[vii]

Family in the Homeland and in the Diaspora

Zubayra Shamseden has three children, who are all politically active although she claims, "I never encouraged them to engage in this work, but it is something they picked up naturally." Her daughter, who studies neuroscience at Harvard, wrote an article on her advocacy work for *The Diplomat*.[viii] Shamseden's husband is also a Uyghur political activist.

After she emigrated from China, Zubayra returned to East Turkestan in 1998, and again in 2001. "My feeling when I traveled back to Ghulja was that my hometown lost its originality and has become a Chinese city. They tore down many old buildings like the library and my high school, pretexting [*sic*] that they were too old, and replaced them with Chinese-style, grey square buildings."

Zubayra acknowledged that, due to her political activities, her family back home is "constantly under pressure." Her brother was sentenced to life in prison for political activities in 1998, and she has lost all contact with the rest of her family since 2015:

> It's a huge burden on me but I don't regret what I am doing, and I will keep doing it. Any human being would do the same I believe. Because what I have done is not just for the sake of my family, it's for the sake of many innocent people. It's not a crisis of just one or two persons, it's a crisis of millions of people. Yes, I do face threats. Everywhere. When I was in Australia, when I was in America, strange things, strange messages—they're always there. Putting pressure on my family members, yes, they are doing it, always threatening them. They've threatened my relatives in East Turkestan. I've heard in different ways that the Chinese government can do anything, wherever we are. So, they have told me many times that if I don't shut up, they can do whatever they want, wherever I am. I heard [from my relatives] that they were very concerned and worried about me, and I told them: "You know, I believe in God. If God is willing, I will die. If not, I will live. So, they don't have to fear. And they don't have to worry about me at all because I am not fearing anything except God."[ix]

Today, Zubayra explains that she values religious schools, which she believes offer a particularly good education. Her own children went to an Islamic College (she does not mention where) and her nephews and nieces were educated in a Catholic college in Australia. She values the fact that these institutions offer a program where religion and secular topics are viewed as mutually compatible, rather than as mutually opposed, "which is how the Chinese authorities always tried to frame things, presenting religious worldviews as totally rejecting science, as inherently backwards." Zubayra explains that her father raised her to see how religion is interrelated to all facets of life and to ideas of humanity, morality, peace, and equality that are at the center of human rights today.

On Islam

Zubayra said she feels very deeply about her religion:

> I think that the devotion and belief is something that is in your heart. Even if a government or someone puts pressure on you or even harms you in some way, that devotion is always in your heart somehow. And that doesn't change. That's my experience. I never changed since I was a child. I learned religion before I went to school. I learned the *Quran*. I never wore the hijab as many Muslim women do because we weren't allowed to look like Muslims. Also, I studied at a Chinese school.
>
> So, that's how I am; that's how I look. But deep in my heart, I believe in God. I deeply live in faith and deeply believe in miracles. Because everything happens with the will of God, and that's what I believe, too. Many times, many people believe that I don't practice Islam because I studied in a Chinese school. And not only me, also my brothers and sisters. Only my sister started to wear a hijab after she came to Australia because it is prohibited and even dangerous to wear it in East Turkestan, especially for families like mine who are "blacklisted families" and are always being watched and have lost so much.
>
> So, because of all these reasons, I look like I am not really practicing, but yes, in reality, I do practice. Especially my devotion. And to me, the devotion comes from the heart. So, if your devotion is in your heart, whatever happens to you, wherever you are, whatever you do, God is with you, and the faith is in your heart, and you should follow that. And that's me.

2. Rushan Abbas

Interviewed on January 22, 2021

Rushan Abbas started her human rights advocacy work while she was a student, co-organizing the pro-democracy demonstrations at Xinjiang University in 1985 and in 1988. Since arriving in the U.S. in 1989, Rushan has played an important role in the diasporic Uyghur community. She was a co-founder and Vice President of the California-based Uyghur Overseas Student and Scholars Association in 1993, the first of its kind in the United States. She was Vice President of the Uyghur

Figure 2 Rushan Abbas. Photographer: Abdulhakim Idris.

American Association in 2000. After Radio Free Asia launched Uyghur service in 1998, Abbas was the first Uyghur reporter broadcasting daily to the Uyghur region. She worked as an interpreter for the U.S. Department of Defense at Guantanamo Bay in 2002 and 2003, and also worked with the HABEAS defense attorney and State Department from 2006 to 2013 on securing the former Guantanamo Uyghurs resettling in the third country. She is currently the Executive Director of the NGO Campaign for Uyghurs which she co-founded in 2017. She frequently briefs U.S. lawmakers and officials on the human rights situation in East Turkistan and regularly appears on media outlets to advocate for the Uyghur cause. Abbas founded the "One Voice One Step" movement and on March 15th, 2018, led simultaneous demonstrations in fourteen countries and eighteen cities to protest China's detention of millions of Uyghurs in concentration camps. She is married to Abdulhakim Idris, Executive Director of Center for Uyghur Studies and author of Menace: China's Colonization of the Islamic World and Uyghur genocide.

Family and Childhood

Rushan Abbas was born in Urumqi in 1967 into a family of intellectuals and professionals. Her mother was a medical doctor who practiced internal medicine at the at Xinjiang University Hospital, where her father also worked as Chair of the Biology Department. The youngest of four siblings, Rushan grew up "spoiled by my siblings, I always got what I wanted."

She recalls growing up during the later period of the Cultural Revolution. Her mother would often tell her the story of how, when Rushan was still a nursing baby, the Red Guard arrived, ready to apprehend her mother: "They did not even wait to let me properly hand the baby over to your grandmother, and they grabbed you so roughly you were screaming." Then the Red Guards shoved the baby at her grandmother and escorted Rushan's mother to the political education center and did not let her return home for two weeks. Her mother recalled, "I could hear your screams in my mind for hours afterwards."

Rushan spent an odd childhood in which family members would suddenly disappear for months. They would be escorted by the police to camps where, as Muslims, they were forcibly educated in the Communist Party's atheistic and nationalistic ideals. Her maternal grandfather was held in detention for three years for being a popular governor of Atush Oblast.

> My baby memories are of hearing about how my grandfather was in jail and was being tortured. My mother often disappeared, then came back. Because of those things that happened to me at a young age, I became aware that our people were treated as second-class citizens in our own Homeland and being persecuted—and I wanted to do something about it. My father used to be taken away for "study sessions." Then they would bring him back, and then take him away again—so that for years he was unable to hold a job.

With the ending of the Cultural Revolution in the mid-1970s, Rushan's father first became the president of Kuytun Agricultural University. Then he was selected as the Chairman of the Xinjiang Science and Academy Association. He was considered *Ping Fan*, an intellectual who had committed no crime.

Student Life at Xinjiang University

In 1984 Rushan enrolled at Xinjiang University where she studied Biology. She became involved in student pro-democracy demonstrations with her close friends and joined in protest demonstrations against the testing of nuclear weapons that were polluting the atmosphere. She recalls, "My grandmother told me about the effects of radiation on the Uyghur population. There were diseases she had never seen before." Also, she remembers a strong enforcement of birth control by the Xinjiang government on the Uyghur women. The government was forcibly sterilizing them after they had their second baby. Rushan and her friends were advocating against forced birth control.

Another issue that concerned her was the transfer of Han Chinese prisoners to East Turkestan. There, they would form gangs and attack Uyghur families.

Rushan described her participation in a major student protest following the death of Mijit Emet, the President of the Student Union on December 8, 1985. Noted for his activism, he had died mysteriously from a "heart attack." Rushan decided to join the close circle of friends of Mijit Emet and try to confront the repressive policies of the Chinese regime. The students decided to honor Mijit Emet and organized a protest. On December 12, 1985, around 15,000–20,000 students from seven different universities marched in the streets of Urumqi, according to Rushan's account. This was Rushan's first involvement in a demonstration. The demonstration of 1985 was also the first student movement in the Chinese territory after the end of the Cultural Revolution. This event made a deep impression on her:

> I will never forget. It was a snowy day and I looked back and could see thousands and thousands of students behind me.

> During my university years, the Uyghurs were in our "Golden Period." In 1979, China was desperate to establish trade relations with the U.S. and trying to get into the Word Trade organization, so they had to show some respect for democracy. Between 1980 and 1990, a ten-year period, we had a lot of freedom. Many of the great Uyghur intellectuals were released from jail. Many were friends with my father and would come to our house. I would sit listening to them talking about what it was like in jail, and what they hoped for hope the future generations. While I was in fifth and sixth grade [age 10–12], because I was the youngest, my parents would take me with them to visit our nationalistic leaders. I would meet and speak with them and listen and ask questions. At that time the government did nothing worse than oblige us to attend political studies every day after classes. My father was an inspiration to me, a role model.

In 1986, Dolkun Isa,[x] the president of the Students Cultural Union of Xinjiang University invited Rushan Abbas to work with him as Vice President. She organized Uyghur cultural events to promote nationalistic ideas and to celebrate "the history our of heroes." Rushan Abbas also founded an organization called "Students Science and Cultural Union." The purpose was to educate and raise awareness among the students of Uyghur history and nationalism.

Entering the Job Market

Rushan spoke of how, after graduating in Biology from Xinjiang University with grades that were consistently first or second in her class, and despite her father's high position in the scientific community, she could not find a job.

> Back then, all the top students were sent by the university to universities or state-owned companies, and I was told I would be sent to Xinjiang Agricultural University to teach. I went there and reported. They accepted me for a teaching position at the plant-pathology department. I had the summer off until September 1, and I was telling everybody about my exciting new job. But when I showed up in September, they took one look at my face and said, "Oh, we don't have a position for *you.*"
>
> I protested, "But you already accepted me and said that I will come back at the end of summer break! I am supposed to teach now.'" Then I found out it was because of my political involvement. Later we learnt that the high-level political officials were asking the Xinjiang Agricultural University president, "Why did you accept her for a teaching position, the daughter of Abbas Borhan?" They were saying, "Didn't you check her political background and her involvement in the protests? She is a troublemaker."
>
> My father was not in Urumqi at that time. He was away for his job. So, I wrote to tell him I am going to my mother's Homeland, where my grandpa was a governor, a town called Atush, near Kashgar. I was hired by a private school that was set up by local Uyghur businessmen, a vocational school where I became a teacher for six months. But my father felt I was in danger and must leave China. He had contacts from being president of the Science and Academy Association and had traveled to the U.S. a couple of times during the mid-1980s. He asked one American professor to sponsor me. He used his influence to get me a passport and a position at Washington State University where I was to pursue a graduate degree in plant pathology.

At the time of Rushan's graduation, in June 1988, when she was 21, the Students Science and Cultural Union organized another protest in Urumqi against the policies of the Chinese authorities. These student protests in Urumqi preceded the 1989 Tiananmen Square protests. Rushan notes:

> When I took the train to Beijing to catch my flight to the U.S., the students were already in Tiananmen Square, protesting. I went there to meet an old friend who was very involved in the demonstration. I came away feeling very encouraged, hoping that something good would happen. Then, shortly after I arrived in the U.S., I watched the breaking news … the military marching in, cracking down on people, killing the students.

Life in the USA

Already experienced and gifted in advocacy work, Rushan continued to pursue her vocation in the U.S. Shortly after her arrival in Washington, D.C., Rushan looked for ways to advocate for the Uyghur people. She approached politicians and wrote articles, hoping to raise awareness of the dire situation of the Uyghurs. She co-founded the California-based Uyghur Overseas Student and Scholars Association in 1993, and served as its first vice president. The charter co-drafted by Rushan Abbas served as the blueprint and played an important role in the establishment of the Uyghur American Association (UAA) in 1998. Rushan was subsequently elected Vice President of UAA for two terms. In 1998, *Radio Free Asia* approached Rushan and invited her to work for its new program, *Uyghur Service*. At the time, Rushan was married and had three children. She and her family lived near Washington State University, where she was majoring in plant pathology. But Rushan felt it was vitally important for the Uyghurs to have a free radio station, so she moved to Washington, D.C., leaving her botanical studies and family behind. After working at *RFA*'s Uyghur Service for three years, Rushan rejoined her family in Fresno, California where she decided to pursue a degree in International Relations.

In 2002, the U.S. Department of Defense invited Rushan to work as an interpreter in Guantanamo Bay. The U.S. had captured twenty-two Uyghurs ("who just happened to be in the wrong place at the wrong time," Rushan explained) in Afghanistan and brought them to Guantanamo Bay as suspected terrorists. Rushan worked as an interpreter for the U.S. Department of Defense at Guantanamo Bay from 2002 to 2003 and again from 2005 to 2013, assisting in the interrogation, exoneration, and resettlement process of these Uyghur prisoners. Her experience at Guantanamo Bay had a significant impact on her future career. Rushan Abbas is currently the Executive Director of *Campaign for Uyghurs*, an NGO which she founded in 2017. She received the 2019 Freedom Fighter Award in recognition of her achievements. In July 2021, *Campaign for Uyghurs* was awarded the World Democracy Courage Tribute and was nominated for the Nobel Peace Prize in 2022. Rushan frequently briefs U.S. lawmakers and officials on the human rights situation in East Turkistan and regularly appears on media outlets to advocate for the Uyghurs.

China's "Hostage Diplomacy" Reprisals on the Abbas Family

Rushan's father, Burhan Abbas, was a renowned Uyghur intellectual and scientist. After the demise of the Cultural Revolution, in 1979 Burhan Abbas became the president of the Xinjiang Science and Technology Association where he authored or published twelve scientific books and established a scientific publishing house in Urumqi. But he was investigated by the political bureau because he hadn't hired any Han people among his 200 employees. Thus, in 1990, when Rushan Abbas started to advocate for Uyghurs' rights, her father, at the age of 59, was summarily dismissed from his position. Rushan interprets this as a retaliation by the Peoples' Republic of China (PRC) to the perceived threat she, his daughter, posed to China through her political activism in the U.S. Rushan explains, "I was active in the U.S., I was approaching lawmakers, and I guess I was being monitored by the Chinese consulate."

In September 2018 Rushan's sister, Dr. Gulshan Abbas, suddenly disappeared only six days after Rushan exposed China's genocidal policies when she participated in a public panel at a "think-tank" in Washington, D.C. In December 2020, Rushan learned that her sister had been sentenced to twenty years in prison on the dubious charge of "terrorism." Rushan believes this punishment of her innocent sister was most likely the Chinese regime retaliating for her advocacy work, since it is a well-known practice of the Chinese authorities to use the family ties of those Uyghurs who speak out in the diaspora to try to silence them. A documentary film "In Search of My Sister," about Rushan's activism and her efforts to locate and rescue her sister was made by Jawad Mir. After her father and sister were targeted due to their association with her, Rushan's commitment to speaking out against China has only intensified. She quit her established successful job as an International Business Director and became a full-time activist and Campaign for Uyghurs has worked tirelessly to raise awareness of the Uyghur genocide and mobilize action. Her organization was instrumental in advocating for and the passage of the Uyghur Human Rights Policy Act and the Uyghur Forced Labor Prevention Act in the U.S. Campaign for Uyghurs was also the founder of the Congressional Uyghur Caucus in the U.S. Congress to further Uyghur issues.

The Political Philosophy and Activism of Rushan Abbas

Rushan Abbas is a charismatic speaker who challenges her audiences with pithy, compelling arguments and sound bites. Like Rebiya Kadeer, Rushan is adept in summarizing and communicating the latest burning issues that arise out of the complex phenomenon of China's genocidal campaign against the Uyghurs. Unlike Rebiya, who speaks in Uyghur with a translator, Rushan is a fluent English speaker.

In the wake of the first media reports about Xinjiang's "re-education camps" in 2017, Rushan initiated a movement to bring Uyghur women around the globe together to participate in global demonstrations called "One Voice, One Step." Her stated purpose was: "All Uyghurs be one voice, and work together with all organizations to end the atrocities."

On March 15, 2018, Uyghurs from eighteen cities in fourteen different countries simultaneously marched in a protest demonstration against Chinese atrocities in their Homeland. The protests in each city were led by Uyghur women. This movement attracted significant attention from the media and many Uyghur women who were involved in these protests continued to engage in Uyghur advocacy afterwards.

When asked what advice she would offer Uyghur women, Rushan replied:

> Women are much stronger and more resilient than men, so never underestimate yourself. Try to make an impact in life, it is so short, so precious. Try not to keep busy with unimportant things, like the once-a-month *chai* [Uyghur women's tea party] where you get ready, get dressed, and so much time is wasted. Use your time for more important things. There are already so many responsibilities in Uyghur culture. Women are supposed to cook, to do housework. It is good to serve your husband and kids, but we all come to this world for a reason, Women raise their sons like our national heroes in the past. What I want to see is every Uyghur family become an institution for educating and raising Uyghur activists and heroes! We don't have a country anymore. We are a minority in our own Homeland now. There are around 10,000 of us in the U.S. but we don't have the population for the younger generations to learn our cultural aspects, about our history. The responsibility, it all falls on us women. We are the first generation to have to fight to learn English, the English culture, and to get a well-paid job in order to create a meaningful life for our children. It is not easy to be a refugee when your country is facing genocide, to compete with native speakers in your work environment, and at the same time to take responsibility for your family. Uyghur women have to step up, to see themselves as the educators but also the voice for people back home facing genocide today.

Two interesting, unexpected things were mentioned in our interview with Rushan Abbas. She confessed she doesn't feel comfortable being called an "activist"; also, that she has always preferred, during her long career in advocacy work, to be the leader's assistant, not the actual leader, who is usually male. Today, however, she is the Executive Director of Campaign for Uyghurs.

When we asked Rushan Abbas what her ultimate goal was, she responded with this thought-provoking statement:

> China is not just about the genocide against Uyghur, it is about the future of the democratic world. China is changing global power, re-establishing slavery, re-establishing dictatorship, and undermining every kind of basic dignity and human rights. So, to me today, fighting for the Uyghurs is about fighting for the future of humanity, for the future of the world.

3. Rahima Mahmut

Interviewed on May 2, 2021 and August 4, 2022

Rahima Mahmut is a singer, translator, and human rights activist. She is the Director of the World Uyghur Congress and Executive Director of Stop Uyghur Genocide in the U.K. She left China in 2000 on a student visa to study at University of Central Lancashire (Preston), and then moved to London. She won the English PEN award for her translation of the 2018 prisoner's memoir, The Land Drenched in Tears by Söyüngül Chanisheff. She has worked extensively with documentary

Figure 3 Rahima Mahmut. Photographer: Zulfukar Ablikim.

filmmakers and television producers as consultant and translator (for example, the ITV documentary, "Undercover: Inside China's Digital Gulag" (2019); and the 2019 BBC documentary, "China: A New World Order"). Currently, she is advisor to the Inter-Parliamentary Alliance on China (IPAC) and has been involved in several high-profile parliamentary campaigns, such as the Genocide Amendment to the Trade Bill, the British Parliament's recognition of the Uyghur genocide, and the diplomatic boycott of the 2022 Beijing Winter Olympics. Rahima is a traditional singer and co-founded the music ensemble, The London Silk Road Collective that regularly performs traditional Uyghur folk and classical music.

Family and Childhood

Rahima Mahmut was born and raised in Ghulja in East Turkestan, in a large religious family. On her mother's side, from her great grandfather on down, the family were all musicians. Her mother sang and played the dutar. Reflecting on her childhood in our interview, Rahima said:

> I was very young when I realized things for Uyghurs were not easy. When my parents and older siblings prayed in our house, they had to lock the gate from inside. My parents would always warn my siblings not to tell anyone we prayed or the police would come and take us away. That was in the later years of the Cultural Revolution. After Mao died, some religious freedom was given back to Uyghurs. The mosques reopened, and my father became an imam in one of the mosques.

Rahima chose to go to Chinese school, against her father's will, because,

> I had started to feel discriminated against by my classmates, but at the time we were a majority in the villages, so the discrimination was in discreet ways, not so open. I found my father [to be] overprotective. So, I chose to live far away. In 1987 went to study petrochemical engineering at Dalian University of Technology in the Ganjingzi District. The university was by the sea, another reason I chose it. At the time, if you had high enough marks, most of your university expenses would be paid for.

Turning Point: Tiananmen Square

After leaving home, Rahima experienced her first turning point. She witnessed the student protest at Tiananmen Square:

> In 1989 I joined a group of students at Dalian University who were engaged in pro-democracy activities. We were demonstrating in May when we heard about the big demonstration in Tiananmen Square. So, we left for Beijing in

mid-May, and I traveled with around 2000 students on a 21-hour train journey. I remember it clearly.

I was there, in Tiananmen Square for two weeks until we received repeated warnings that the military would come in on the 4th of June and crack down on the demonstrators. So, we left the square on the 2nd of June and took the train back to the Ganjingzi District.

On the 4th of June I was already back at Dalian University, and the students were summoned to the big hall to watch the news on television about Tiananmen Square. We were in shock to see how the news was completely distorted. We knew how peaceful that demonstration was, but we saw how the tanks had come in and killed thousands of students. That was a very important moment for my activism because that event gave me a deeper understanding of how the Chinese government works—their ruthlessness ... that they would kill the best and the brightest of young Chinese people as well as the ethnic groups! That was an important turning point. Tiananmen Square shaped my ideology and my understanding of this ruthless regime.

Facing Discrimination

Rahima's second turning point involved her experiences with discrimination in the job market and the workplace:

Then, on graduating from Dalian University in 1992 with a top degree, I could not find a job in Urumqi, in the Capital—while other students who were Han Chinese and had just come to the city were hired immediately. Later, I heard they were recruited by a team, a working group, who were scouting the top students for jobs at the universities across mainland China. Han students were given extra incentives and encouragement to come to East Turkestan and get jobs. There was a big boom of factories being set up in the Xinjiang Autonomous region due to the rich gas resource. One of my classmates got a job in a petrochemical plant, but he was the only Uyghur there.

When we asked Rahima, "Did you feel that, as a woman, you were being discriminated against?" she replied, "Women are generally discriminated against in Science, there is less opportunity to get a top job, but I believe that other Han Chinese females who had the same degree as me had got jobs easily. I wanted to be a teacher in the petrochemical university in Urumqi. They needed five teachers that year, but they refused to take me." She concluded:

So that was a big disappointment. I spoke Mandarin like my mother tongue, I spoke English as well, I had obtained my degree in petrochemical engineering from one of top ten universities in China, and yet I could not find my dream job. So, in the end I took a job in a petrochemical town and worked in an Ethylene plant. After taking this job I worked from 1992 to 1996. It was Hell! My experience was Hell. From day one there was severe discrimination, despite the fact that I was qualified and spoke the language perfectly, they were always trying to find fault and give Uyghurs a hard time.

Then in 1996 I became a teacher in a petrochemical college that trained technicians. Returning to my college in 1998, I received an offer to study hotel management at Guangdong University of Business Studies. The college had decided to set up a new course because tourism very becoming popular.

Turning Point: The Ghulja Incident

Rahima identifies her major turning point was when she witnessed the Ghulja Incident, also known as the Ghulja Massacre:

> But the main reason I made the decision to leave my country was because of what happened on February 5, 1997—the Ghulja protest. It was the most important event that affected me—the terror I witnessed in the aftermath, with the police raiding the houses, taking away thousands of young people.
>
> I was visiting my mother with my son who was a year and a half old. There had been protests in downtown Ghulja that day. In the evening we learned that over 100 were killed at gunpoint. Then, from that night, they started raiding house to house to try to catch all the protestors who fled from the scene. I was visiting my mother, so I heard about protests taking place. Then, later, the government brought the military in, surrounded the demonstration and opened fire, killing around 100 protesters, mainly young people. I was not at the scene but word travels quickly by word of mouth, and Ghulja is a close community, so when something happens, everyone knows.
>
> My family was ok, but my relatives, those who participated in the protest and two of my friends were all arrested and got ten-year prison sentences. Another family member was given twelve years, so almost every household was affected. Ghulja is a small town, if you have four or five thousand arrested, either your neighbor or your family member—someone you know—it has a big impact on the community. Children grow up without fathers. They cannot forget that!
>
> After they had fired on the protestors, from that night on February 5th, they started raiding, house to house to house, trying to catch all the protesters who had fled from the scene. Up to four or five thousand Uyghurs, mainly young males, were arrested, and many of my neighbors and relatives were taken away afterwards. Ghulja suddenly became a most terrifying place! And I witnessed with helplessness how everyone felt.

The Chinese government twisted the protest, which was very peaceful, with students demanding cultural and religious freedom, but the government claimed it was a violent uprising of terrorists. There had just been three-month period—a crackdown that started with the government detaining mainly young clerics. And so this protest was a demand for their release. Also, they had targeted a cultural practice that was very popular in Ghulja called *meshrep*, which was now banned. So, because of these reasons, the people took to the street demanding their constitutional rights! The Chinese Constitution actually gives us the right to have our culture and religious freedom.

So, 1997, in my opinion, that was the turning point for me. It was maybe the biggest crackdown in the region since the Cultural Revolution. I vowed if I could find any opportunity to leave my country, I would take it.

Rahima also told the story of another turning point; of how she was turned away from hotels because she was Uyghur.

In 1989, when I was teaching at my college, Guangdong University of Business Studies, I was offered an opportunity to study hotel management because the college had decided to set up a new department. Tourism and hotel management had become very popular subjects, and I was offered a chance to teach that, along with English. So, I went to Guangzhou to take the course. Meanwhile, I had already applied to the University of Lancashire in the U.K. and had been offered a bursary.

In 1998, when I traveled to Guangzhou from Urumqi on my way to a conference, I had to change trains in Zhengzhou. Stranded in Zhengzhou that evening, I could not find a hotel to sleep in before catching the next train in the morning. I went to the five different hotels near the train station, and not one hotel would allow me to stay, even after I showed my teacher's certificate. "We don't accept anyone from your background," the receptionists would tell me.

And that was another terrible experience I had as a Uyghur. In the end, even when I showed my teacher's certificate—at the fifth hotel (it was after midnight)—the receptionist said, "We cannot accept you." I was so upset I started almost shouting, so she called the manager. I reasoned with him. I said, "Look, I teach people like you to become hotel managers. I am a teacher, how dare you discriminate against me!"

Eventually, they allowed me to stay, but I had to promise to leave the hotel at the crack of dawn so no one would see me. I had to fight to stay one night in this hotel! Actually, if I were doubting whether or not I should leave my country, if I had any doubts about leaving, that event made me feel very strongly that I did not want to live any longer in that country!

So, I left in 2000. I managed to get a visa to go and do a master's degree in environmental management in the U.K., and I received a bursary for the course. I arrived in England in September 2000, and I never went back to China.

Becoming a Political Activist in London

Rahima spoke about how she built her career as a political activist after completing her degree in Manchester and moving to London.

> My main reason for coming to the U.K. was to speak up for my people. From Day One since I arrived, I have been talking about the Uyghurs—who we are, what is happening in China. I was surprised when I first came to the U.K.—I thought English people knew about the Uyghur people. I would say, "I am Uyghur, from East Turkestan or Xinjiang." People would just stare at me. They didn't know what I was talking about.
>
> After I came to London in 2002, I started to work with refugees, doing interpreting and translation work. In 2004 I co-founded a music ensemble, originally called The London Uyghur Ensemble [since renamed, The SOAS Silk Road Collective]. Through music we try to raise awareness of the Uyghur people's existence and culture and to educate people about our beautiful musical tradition.
>
> I joined the Tibetan movement and the Chinese democratic movement with many other NGOs, to try to reach out to the U.K. government and the general public. Also, I work as an interpreter for Uyghur refugees. I translated a memoir called *The Land Drenched in Tears* in 2016 that won the English PEN award for the best translation. All my work, everything I do, is very much about my people and the Uyghur cause.
>
> Since 2017, when these atrocities at the "re-education" camps started to be reported in the international media, my workload has become huge. I have worked with many journalists and with filmmakers on different documentaries. Among them I can mention *Inside China's Digital Gulag*, which won a BAFTA award, an Emmy Award, and other awards. I worked as a consultant and interpreter, also on a 2020 BBC documentary, *China the New World Order*, and *The Search for the Missing*, interviewing the victims, translating testimonies, and helping with subtitles. This latest BBC news report about the systematic rape in the camps, I have been working since October on that, and did the voiceover.

We asked her if she ever found her work upsetting or traumatic.

> Although I have been tough, my job is not easy. It's horror. I live very closely with the victims, I translate the details of their tortures, the intention is to do what is best to get the story out so the world will know what is happening, and then act. I started my post as project director of the World Uyghur Congress in August 2019. In the past, I was working voluntarily, but since taking over this position with the WUC, it is almost a full-time job. Now my work is focused on the campaign with the English parliament.

The reason I have been so passionately involved in my work is because I have been trying to reveal the truth, even though it is so painful for us to watch our own brothers and sisters give such horrific details about what they have been through. But I feel it is necessary. Only when the world learns the truth will they act. To translate accurately, you have to rewind, every few seconds, I would record my own voice saying what they said, as if it were me. So I have to become numb. We interviewed six people, ten hours of translation, every interview lasted one hour, one and a half hours. I had to translate every line—but in end the BBC only used two or four lines. But we can use the information for other occasions, like The Uyghur Tribunal, with permission from the BBC.

We asked Rahima how she manages to juggle all her Uyghur advocacy projects.

I started my post as director of the World Uyghur Congress in August 2019. Since I started working, in the past I was working voluntarily, but now I am taking over this position almost full time. Also, I am in charge of the "Stop Uyghurs Genocide" campaign in the U.K.

Since 2019 this "Genocide Amendment to the Trade Bill" has been a focus of the U.K. government and the public. We have achieved great support from MPs as well as from communities. The Jewish community is finally behind the campaign, and the Muslim Council of Britain. I have been working with Sir Geoffrey Nice and Lord Alton on the bill. After a debate in Parliament, the first bill was presented to the House of Lords and it passed—but then in the House of Commons it was narrowly defeated. So we made changes to the bill last week in the House of Lords, then it is going back to the House of Commons this month, and we are lobbying to get as many MPs as possible to support this bill. We believe there is a genocide happening in East Turkestan. There is no court available, the international routes are blocked. So now we have started a campaign called "Stop Uyghur Genocide." So much is going on here and my workload, it is very difficult for me.

We asked Rahima if she and her fellow activists felt they had made any progress.

Every country has its own trade policies with a state that is involved with crimes against humanity. Only when you have that legal definition of genocide can you force governments to stop trade with China, to use sanctions. Words are very strong in governments, but actions are very little. Only when the world acts against China it might be possible for China to change its behavior. When the BBC News came out about rape in the camps, China created its own news and said it was all lies. You can see the truth is hurting.

The Next Generation

Rahima spoke about her son who lives in London, and their close relationship:

Aside from his full-time job in finance, my son runs a popular network for Uyghur youth. He was one of the co-founders of *Tarim Network*, and the goal of the organization is to connect, inspire and unite the younger Uyghur generation. For example, my son is leading a project on the Uyghur language curriculum. I had a virtual concert in Australia last year, and *Tarim* hosted the event. He is very different from me in the way he does his work, very discreet, he doesn't like to promote himself. He supports my work, he always tells me how proud he is of me. He wouldn't call himself an "activist," but to him "success" means our people gaining their freedom. I gave him complete freedom, I never asked him to get involved—but this situation, what is happening now, it really has awakened the conscience of our youth. But my son brings the cause to the attention of the world in a softer way. Now I know that someone will take over my work if something happens to me.

My son visited my old country in 2012, where he was detained at the airport for three hours. He wasn't free, he had to register with the police on arrival, and report to them wherever he travelled, so he saw the suffocating control that was there.

It was very different for him because he was here in the U.K. since he was seven, and no one would dare to ask to go through your phone in this country without reason. But in my country, the first thing they took was his phone and checked all his messages. He felt very uncomfortable. I warned him, "Stay calm, don't raise your voice and you will be fine. You have a British passport, and you are young." My brother dropped him off at the airport five hours before his return flight, just in case they decided to question him. And he almost missed his flight!

It is so important to experience something directly just once. It stays with you all your life. My son lived with his cousin for two years before he came to the U.K. Her father had been arrested in Ghulja, so she grew up without a father. My son lived with his grandparents and was close friends with the neighbor's son, whose father had been arrested, accused of organizing the Ghulja protests and executed. My son remembers all those terrible things that happened in Ghulja, and how the children must grow up without fathers.

We asked Rahima if she had any specific goals for the future:

I am not a politician—I am just an activist in the struggle for Uyghur human rights. Our most urgent demand at the moment is to get governments to recognize the genocide and fulfill their responsibilities under the Genocide

Convention. This way, we hope to pressure the Chinese government to close the camps and to release all those people who are detained illegally. Also, the [Uyghur] children—release those children to their own families! These are the most pressing issues. Also, for people like myself, lift the ban on telephone calls so we can call our families. I haven't spoken to my sisters or brothers since January 2017—and the majority of Uyghurs living abroad are suffering. We demand our constitutional right to practice our religion, our own culture, to choose what we eat or do not eat. We should never be forced to eat pork. In 1955 it was agreed that so-called "Xinjiang" was an Autonomous Region. But China has never honored that autonomy. Our ultimate goal, for the long term, is freedom from China's oppression. We should have power to make our own decisions, politically, economically, in our way of life. We are just human beings like all other human beings.

4. Rukiye Turdush

Interviewed on February 21, 2021

Figure 4 Rukiye Turdush. Photographer: Berkalp Birlik.

Rukiye Turdush is perhaps the most prominent female Uyghur activist in Canada, and a prolific writer. Born in Ghulja, East Turkestan, she received her primary and secondary education in local Uyghur schools. After graduating from high school, she left her Homeland to study Mandarin Chinese for two years at Beijing Minzu University. She obtained her bachelor's degree in Chinese history from Shanghai Eastern Normal University in 1994. Rukiye arrived in Canada in 1998 with her father, husband, and infant son, speaking only Uyghur and Chinese. She taught herself English, and in 2007 she obtained a B.A. in International Relations from the University of Windsor and a postgraduate degree in Social Work from George Brown College. In 2020 she received a postgraduate degree in International Law and Multipolar Diplomacy from Catalonia University in Spain. Since 2018 she has been working as a social worker. As a main contributor to the Uyghur Research Institute, she is often invited to speak at Canadian universities. A prolific writer, she has published three books and numerous academic articles and newspaper op-eds. She is a founder of the Center for East Turkistan National Interest that was established in Canada in 2022. She is also the current President of East Turkistanian Federation of Canada.[xi]

Childhood and Family

Growing up in Ghulja, Rukiye says she was unaware of ethnic discrimination against the Uyghurs:

> I grew up in a Uyghur neighborhood with a Uyghur school and Uyghur kids. I would see one or two Chinese persons on the streets, consider them as new immigrants. I did not know about social injustices as I was a child.

Rukiye's situation reflects an era when the Uyghur were the dominant population of East Turkestan. Han Chinese migration to Xinjiang began in the early 1990s, a shift that she herself would later witness.[xii]

During her university years, Rukiye began to experience an increasing tension, motivated by Chinese prejudice against Uyghurs. In 1988, after graduating from high school at age 16, Rukiye was sent to Beijing Minzu University to study Mandarin Chinese for two years. During this time she received excellent exam results. While in Beijing, she mostly interacted with other Uyghur and Turkic students. When her two-year language program was completed, she felt obliged to major in a B.A on Chinese history, because Uyghur students were assigned mandatory subjects to study, and they had very limited choices. This prompted her to ask herself an important question: "Why am I going to study Chinese history? There is nothing related to me in it. It is not my history; it is not world history. I really was not interested in it."

At Shanghai Normal University, Rukiye shared a dormitory with Chinese female students and found she was the only Uyghur student in her class. She notes, "In those four years I realized that they were so different, and they realized that I was so different as well. We are different people. When I was a kid, I never differentiated between nationalities or ethnicities."

This tension led to a confrontation with a Chinese student who showed her a classical Chinese poem, "Han Chinese are your Masters since Long Ago," and claimed the author was Uyghur. The Chinese student read the poem out loud to her, then commented, "See? Still today you are coming to our universities to receive education from us."

Rukiye retorted, "I did not want to come here; if I had a country, I would never have come here!"

The Chinese student shouted, "Oh! Your East Turkestan separatist idea is very strong!"

Rukiye responded, "So what? You guys have controlled my country that is why I don't have a country. And I don't believe that the author of that poem was a Uyghur; a Uyghur does not have a name like Yuan. That is a fake history. Chinese history is all fake. That is why I don't want to study it. I hate it!"

Rukiye recalls that a "big fist fight" ensued after this verbal exchange. As the result of that incident, Rukiye was transferred to a dormitory occupied by local Shanghai students. She found Shanghai people "less overtly racist" towards the Uyghurs; more apolitical and Westernized, nevertheless, she continued to experience other conflicts with fellow students.

Rukiye describes experiencing an "identity crisis" during her student years in Shanghai. She notes: "My hair is dark brown and a little bit curly, but I liked black hair and a white face and when you put red lipstick it looks nice."

So, she dyed her hair black and cut it in similar in style to that of Hong Kong film stars. Her Shanghai classmates loved it, but her mother scolded her: "You make me feel suffocated! Why do you cover your forehead like a Chinese? You look so ugly, just like a Chinese girl!"

Rukiye felt confused: "My mother loved me to have long hair, she loved to make a variety of Uyghur braid hairstyles."[xiii]

Years later, she understood why her mother had scolded her:

I came to the realization that I needed to accept my Uyghur identity and grow my hair long again. They [Han Chinese] want us to be like them. They don't like diversity. They consider themselves as the superior nation. All textbooks depicting any other system rather than Chinese governance and Chinese ideology as evil. This narrative breeds doubt and fosters a profound sense of *ennui* in me towards the educational textbooks at the school. Also, a perpetual sense of longing engulfs me, stemming from the stark reality of being detached from my own community and family, residing with Han Chinese students. Although, there were instances of thinking that maybe imitating the appearances and mannerism around me would grant me equal treatment and alleviate the lingering feeling of incompleteness. Yet, those moments swiftly dissolved into the abyss, for I couldn't shake the profound realization that I embraced a pride in being true to myself and being Uyghur. My parents share my discontent, well aware of the longstanding conflict with Han Chinese since the Chinese invasion.

During her university career, Rukiye challenged China's "official" revisionist history of East Turkestan. "Xinjiang has not been an Inseparable Part of China,"[xiv] was the title of her final paper for her Chinese history major at Shanghai Normal University. Her paper challenged the Chinese government's claim that the ancestors of the Uyghurs moved from Mongolia or Western Asia to Xinjiang, which had long been controlled and home to the Chinese since ancient times, long before the Uyghurs arrived. She notes that she had always doubted this version of history:

> Uyghurs have a big population and a big land, so how come they never have had a country? How come we have become an inseparable part of China? How stupid were my ancestors? Why did they not do anything and just become part of somebody else?

In her last semester, Rukiye decided to explore this question. After searching the library, she discovered a book called *Kashgaria* written by Kuropatkin (1882), a history of the hero Yaqup Beg, who rebelled against the Qing government and established an independent Kashgarian state which lasted for ten years (1866–77) in the Uyghur region.[xv] Citing this book in her paper, she argued that Uyghurs had established an independent state in recent history. She recalls how she felt, "That was a great paper. I was proud of it."

But her professor, an elderly man who did his Ph.D. in the U.S., summoned her to his home for a talk. He rebuked her, saying, "You have studied here for four years, and you learn this garbage? You came here for nothing. What is this?"

Rukiye tried to defend her paper, arguing: "But I have proof. Did you not read my paper? Xinjiang has not always been an inseparable part of China. You are an academic, why are you talking like this?"

Her professor told her that she was "poisoned," contaminated by erroneous ideas. But because she was so young, he would not report her to the university, otherwise, she would have been expelled or even sent to jail. He ordered her to destroy the paper and never mention this incident to anyone.

Tensions in the Workplace

When Rukiye returned to Urumqi she was struck by the differences between her region and Shanghai. She was turned away in her job search because of her Uyghur ethnicity, but after a few months was hired as a journalist through a family "connection" [her father bribed someone]. She worked at a newspaper agency amongst Chinese employees who were a great deal less educated than her, but who were her superiors. On her way to work she often witnessed Chinese police targeting Uyghur youth on the streets.

Part of her work was visiting and reporting on local colleges. She noticed that Uyghur colleges lacked heating systems and relied on coal for heating which produced smoke—an unhealthy environment for young students—while the Chinese colleges had central heating and were fully equipped with modern appliances. Moreover, Uyghur colleges were using outdated 1970s textbooks while the Chinese colleges had updated textbooks sent directly from Beijing. Rukiye notes:

> This is why these young Uyghurs could not be excellent and could not find jobs after finishing school. Most kids in these schools are from Uyghur farming families. Their parents sell their land, their sheep, to support their children's education, but it is useless.

She published an article on this problem in the agency's newspaper. The Communist Party Secretary of the agency asked her to stop distributing the newspapers. He argued: "This is going to harm the reputation of CCP if you say Uyghur kids are learning from outdated textbooks. This is going to create ethnic hatred and ruin the CCP's reputation."

Rukiye responded: "But this is the truth! You guys have to change."

He retorted: "You are very young, you don't understand." Then he ordered the distribution of the newspaper in which her article was published to be stopped immediately.

In this article, she also compared the conditions of Uyghur and Chinese schools; exposing the inferior heating systems, poorly equipped dormitories, and meager facilities in the Uyghur schools. She tried to convince the Party Secretary. But he advised her:

> If the CCP is right, we should say it is right. Even if the Communist Party is wrong, we still have to say it is right. Why are you so critical? Where did you learn this? We don't know what kind of education you got in Shanghai, but we think you will have to receive a political education here.

This frustrating situation led Rukiye to quit the newspaper and become a teacher. After much discussion, she was transferred to a school where she was required to teach courses in Marxist Philosophy and Ethnic Problems. In the final exam her students had to answer the following question: "Should we oppose Uyghur nationalism or Chinese chauvinism? Should we be against Uyghur nationalism only?" Around 800 Uyghur students from three regions of Xinjiang wrote the exam and most of them answered that they should also oppose Chinese chauvinism. This created a scandal in the school. The school's Party Secretary announced that this situation would be reported to the Public Security Department of Xinjiang and that all students who gave the "wrong" answer would be instantly expelled from their schools. But Rukiye protested it was her responsibility and that the students should not be blamed as she had taught them to think this way. The school authorities finally decided to "soften" the repercussions. Rukiye was dismissed from her teaching post and she and her students were required to attend political study ("indoctrination sessions" as she explained). Anyone who refused would be sent to jail.

The Turning Point: The Attack on Her Brother

In the early 1990s Chinese migration to Ghulja was on the rise. Rukiye recalls buses filled with Chinese migrants arriving in the city—poor, under-educated people desperate to improve their lives. She describes the scene as follows:

> It used to take four days to travel by train from Beijing to our region, but then the fast train came in the early 1990s. I grew up seeing very few Chinese people, but my family lived near the big bus station, and we realized in 1992 that a lot of Chinese were starting to come to East Turkestan. They would get off the bus carrying only a backpack, a blanket, and some of them holding a child. The government was giving 30,000 Yuan to any Chinese willing to migrate to Xinjiang, so migrant settlers were pouring into the Uyghur region. When they arrived in Ghulja, they made a very bad impression on the local Uyghurs.

> My brother was eighteen and he was upset. He was thinking it was a pollution; too many people spitting everywhere; when they ate, they left garbage; and they were taking all the jobs. Before, Ghulja was a beautiful city, it didn't look like the rest of East Turkestan. Everybody had a garden in front of the door and blue and white painted houses, beautiful tree-lined streets and it was very clean. We had lot of water, so it is a green city, not like in the south. But then the settlers come,

they make a mess, they throw garbage around and they eat everything. They would knock on your door and ask, "Can I catch the frogs from your garden? They can be a good meal." They think the frogs have an owner! And each time it rains the earthworms come out, and they pick up all the earthworms and eat them. My grandmother was very upset because the earthworms break up the soil so that vegetables and flowers can grow. She said they were destroying the garden. She complained the soil became very hard, and the plants could not flourish.

My brother lived with my grandmother, and they were talking, "Why do they eat everything?" she said. "They are killing all the birds and we can no longer hear them sing, and they eat all the frogs, so it is silent in the evening and invites so many mosquitoes."

The government was sending all the criminals, all the poor people to East Turkestan. They had no culture, no education, so what they brought us was pollution. As a child I used to watch the worms when it rained, my grandmother told me, "Don't touch them they soften the soil, it helps our garden." They [the settlers] would knock on her door and ask my grandmother, "Can we pick your worms?" She said no and kicked them out. It was bad for her flowers. Because they eat frogs, so many mosquitos came that bring diseases.[xvi]

"They even ate my dog," added Rukiye. "But that is another story …"

Rukiye described how this worsening situation led to her brother's rebellion and to his violent demise:

My brother was so upset so he put a bracket [barrier] on the highway. And stopped the bus with his three friends. He told the bus driver "you can't enter the city, go back to where you come from." So, for two days no buses could come. No police came, but on the third day around 400 Chinese men came from the XPCC (Xinjiang Production and Construction Corps, 4th Division)[xvii]—they were civil soldiers—they all had big knives, and they attacked my brother and his friends. One friend was injured, the other two friends ran away, but my brother didn't run. On the other side of the street there was a bazaar where people were selling fabric and apples, but when they saw the mob coming, they all ran away. There was a man called Kamal and he called to my brother to run, but he refused. Kamal saw him fighting and he was killed by the mob. They stabbed him with big knives. After he fell down, the mob ran towards the neighborhood to attack other Uyghurs on the street. Then, someone took him to a hospital, but doctors failed to save his life. That was in 1992. He was only 18.

Second Turning Point: The Ghulja Incident[xviii]

Rukiye described how she witnessed the aftermath of the 1997 Ghulja Incident:

China strictly controlled the information, so I didn't have any idea what was happening. We heard on TV that a bad mob had descended on Ghulja, that they were separatists, but [the government] didn't show anything, and they blocked the roads to Ghulja so people couldn't travel. After five months when they opened the road, I went. There were checkpoints everywhere, the police were so rude, they get into the bus and look so scary. They say to everyone who looks Uyghur, "Get out, get out!" You are getting up, walking out, and they hit you, throw your luggage! I was so insulted, I was crying. The bus had seven or eight Uyghur men. At every checkpoint they held two or three of them there. I could speak Chinese, I could argue with them, so they don't treat me so badly, but many of the Uyghur passengers didn't speak Mandarin. None of the young Uyghur men were left in the bus by the time we arrived in Ghulja.

My cousin came to pick me up. The streets were full of army trucks, I was looking at them, and she said, "Don't look!" We just walked looking at the ground until we came to my grandmother's home. I secretly visited my friends early in the morning, using the small back streets of Ghulja (the army trucks all stayed on the big streets). One of my girlfriends had three brothers who were all arrested, the youngest was 14 years old. Another friend also had brothers arrested. They were so scared they couldn't speak to me. They were afraid of surveillance, or spies. All of our male classmates were gone, they told me, there were none left. They had all disappeared at the time of the Ghulja demonstration in 1997.

Immigrating to Canada

The events in Ghulja in 1997 prompted Rukiye to make the difficult decision to leave China and emigrate to the U.S. She describes how she and her father mistakenly ended up immigrating to Canada:

I asked my dad to get me a student visa at the U.S. Embassy, I didn't know much about Canada at that time. He mistakenly went to the Canadian Embassy in Beijing and a man at the door gave him a business immigrant form. When he entered the Embassy, an officer explained to him that Canada was a free country, no different than the U.S.A. I was married at that time. The officer first encouraged my father to apply for a business immigrant visas, but after knowing he didn't know English, the officer told him, "you will go bankrupt if you go to Canada as a business immigrant because you don't know English." After hearing this, my father just left. Then, I told the officer in Chinese, "I want to go to Canada! I grew up in this country in just one system, I want to see Western culture. I don't want to live and die like this." The officer said, "Call your father and let me talk with my boss." My mother was outside arguing with my father in front of the embassy, saying, "They keep arresting my sons! They already killed one of them! Go back!" So, she [and] my father went back inside and the officer said, "in Vancouver, Chinese is the second language, so your daughter can be a translator for you, and she can learn English at the same time."

While her family was being screened for immigration to Canada, an officer asked Rukiye for her views on the Ghulja Incident. She replied that she would fully support those Uyghurs who engaged in peaceful protest; that their voices were legitimate. Hearing this, her family members were worried because the translator was Chinese. However, the officer said that Canada needed honest people like her and granted them immigrant visas. "Welcome to Canada!" he said. Reflecting upon her visit to the Canadian Embassy in Beijing, Rukiye said, "I am indebted to that officer in countless ways, yet I never had a chance to find him and express my gratitude."

While Rukiye was staying in Beijing to finalize the immigration process, she found herself and her infant son repeatedly turned away from Beijing hotels because of her ethnicity. The night before her flight she managed to find a hotel room, but she was abruptly woken up in the early hours by soldiers in uniform. She recounts: "Chinese soldiers—not the police—burst into the hotel room and my baby started to scream. The soldiers held me at gunpoint while they searched the room and then they evicted us."

Rukiye arrived in Vancouver at age 26 with her father and former husband in 1998, but she did not like the city because it was full of Chinese people. She describes how her husband discovered there were two Uyghurs in Montreal, so they moved there. "I had to learn French, I had a little baby, did not speak the language, couldn't get a job. We had a very difficult time and did not get much help."

After her mother joined them in Montreal, Rukiye assisted her father in running his business affairs. She did this for five years, but then decided to go to university. She had to explain to her father that she did not come to Canada just to make money; she wanted to speak out for Uyghurs. "I had to educate myself in order to help my people. I don't know what's happening to them. I had to do something."

Despite strong opposition from her parents who felt she should enroll in dental hygiene or nursing, she enrolled in the University of Windsor to study International Relations. In 2007 she obtained a bachelor's degree in Social

Work. That same year, she moved to Washington, D.C. to work for the famous Uyghur activist Rebiya Kadeer at the International Uyghur Human Rights and Democracy Foundation. A year later she returned to Canada.

Rukiye then decided to move to Toronto where she served as the President of the Canadian Uyghur Society for four years. During this period, she organized numerous media events, conferences, seminars, and protests, collaborating with many other organizations. Her Twitter account has more than 15,000 followers.[xix]

Despite her impressive track record, Rukiye Turdush made it quite clear in our interview that she dislikes being called an "activist":

> I hate it when people call me an "activist." Activism should not be considered a formal occupation or job but rather a fundamental and instinctive reaction that arises within each person when they see the injustices in this world. Activism is a natural and inherent quality that should be present in all individuals rather than being limited as a specific profession to a group of people … Millions of people are, in this moment, suffering in the camps, so how could we not do anything? It is impossible to tolerate it. This is me, this is my people, you don't have to choose to speak up, it is a natural human response, it is everybody's duty. I live in a free country. That is the most beautiful value and advantage of Canada and other Western countries. When I am using that advantage, people think I am an activist. We can have freedom to fight China here in Canada, but I can't *do* anything, only with words not actions. Sometimes I feel useless, ashamed at being here when so many people have died. Every day I watch TikTok videos, read the news and I can't do anything. I am still dressing up, doing my make up, eating, walking like a human, pretending nothing is happening. I feel shame, so much shame for being human!

Today Rukiye Turdush is an outspoken critic of what she perceives as Canada's apathy regarding the plight of the Uyghurs. She and other Uyghurs openly criticized Canada's passive acceptance of China's bullying and "hostage diplomacy" during the "Two Michaels" crisis.[xx] She has written many articles in which she urged Canada to take a lead in recognizing China's treatment of the Uyghurs as a genocide.[xxi] She urges Canada to play a more important role in the United Nations and to put pressure on the U.N. to launch a serious, unbiased investigation of China's treatment of the Uyghurs. Rukiye has criticized the Trudeau government for its indecisive response to the 2020–21 Meng Wanzhou extradition crisis and to the 2005 arrest of Huseyin Celil, a Uyghur Canadian who is serving a extrajudiciary life sentence in a Chinese prison.[xxii] Rukiye argues that Canada's weak responses have encouraged Beijing to pressure and manipulate Canada in many diplomatic exchanges.

The "Long Arm" of China

On February 11, 2019, while speaking at Ontario's McMaster University, Rukiye was interrupted by a shouting Chinese student. She was addressing the plight of over a million Muslim Uyghurs. During her talk, Turdush had spotted a Chinese man in the audience who was filming her and making faces. When she was interviewed by the CBC, Rukiye said she did not object to being filmed as it was not a closed-door event, but the man's sarcastic smile and hateful expression made her uncomfortable. When it was time for the hour-long question-and-answer session, she asked the Chinese student if he had any questions, to which he replied "no." Rukiye then asked the man what he thought about the presentation. "He just [repeated] a few words: 'You! McMaster, you! No right speak!' [which Rukiye took to mean that he disapproved of her speaking at the university]." Footage of the incident shows the man speaking in broken English, and saying the F-word before leaving. Rukiye commented: "You see, this is the typical Chinese behavior that is controlled by the Chinese government."[xxiii]

5. Arzu Gul

Interviewed on February 14, 2021

Arzu Gul was born in Korla, East Turkestan and worked in village governments in her city. She left China in 2002 to join her husband who was studying in Sweden, and they arrived in Canada in 2008. Arzu Gul began her activist work in 2017 after reading media reports of Xinjiang's "re-education" camps. She has connected Uyghur human rights activists with various community organizations and arranged meetings with influential politicians to raise awareness about the Uyghur issue at the community and government levels. Despite China's efforts to eradicate Uyghur culture and Islamic teachings, Arzu Gul has dedicated her time to ensuring the preservation of the Uyghur language and culture by hosting community lessons and events. She was the founder of the Canadian Uyghur Learning Centre in Toronto, which offers courses in Uyghur language and culture for Uyghur women and children. Since the pandemic started, she has been focusing on online teachings. She spoke up for the release of prisoner Huseyin Celil at the "A Call To End Genocide" event on July 17, 2021. Arzu Gul volunteers for CSRDN (Canadians in Support of Refugees in Dire Need) to raise awareness of the Uyghurs' situation, working with a team of Muslims, Jews, Christians, and Falun Gong practitioners who are trying to expose and ban the lucrative practice of human organ harvesting in China.

Figure 5 Arzu Gul. Photographer: Yasin Mamatjan.

Childhood and Family

Arzu Gul was born in a village near Korla city in East Turkestan in the early 1970s into a family of farmers. She grew up with four brothers. She was the youngest in the family and describes her childhood as happy. She recounts:

> We had many visitors who would bring us gifts. My father was proud of me and gave me self-confidence. I felt I could do anything. I was a favorite of my teachers, and usually had the highest marks in the class. We grew vegetables, we had beautiful pear trees and an apricot orchard, and we planted corn and cotton.

Arzu attended a local Uyghur middle school, but she gained a high score in her university entrance exam and was awarded a scholarship to go to Nankai University, one of the top universities in China, to do a bachelor's degree in economics.[xxiv] In 1990, she arrived at Nankai University in Tianjin City and was struck by the economic disparity between her home town and the eastern Chinese region with its tall buildings and shopping malls. The Nankai University she attended in 1990 was much better equipped than Xinjiang University, she recalls: "We used computers that were not available in Xinjiang."

Tensions in University Studies

As a Uyghur student living among Chinese, Arzu encountered daily incidents of discrimination while walking on the streets of Tianjin. She recounts how:

> I was often mistaken as a foreigner by the Chinese, but when they realized I was Uyghur, they would say, 'Oh, you are Xinjiang girl' in a derogatory tone. They held the stereotypical view that Uyghurs are backward, barbaric, and that many of them are petty criminals or thieves.[xxv]

Arzu became close friends with a Chinese student, who would come shopping with her. "She was my shield. She liked Uyghur people, she thought they were beautiful and kind."

Arzu rode a bicycle to avoid harassment while in buses and on crowded streets. She explains:

> Many Chinese men can't find a girl to marry so when they see a young girl on the bus, they will touch her. In any public area that is crowded, there would be men touching [molesting] women. These men are not healthy mentally, and because we [Uyghur girls] look different they feel they can touch you. It would happen everywhere, even in the university library. I hated it! So, I bought a bicycle to avoid crowded streets and transport.

She described an unpleasant situation of sexual harassment:

> One Uyghur girl in my dorm came to me in private crying because she had been sexually harassed by a man on an overly crowded bus, and she was worried about getting pregnant from the incident, because a Chinese man had been rubbing himself against her and made a mess all over her dress, so she had to get off from the bus long before her reaching her destination.

Arzu spoke of how Uyghur women are exploited to lure Chinese settlers to Xinjiang: "The government uses pictures of Uyghur girls to encourage Chinese men to move to Xinjiang. The ads would say how beautiful and kind they are, what hard-working wives they make."

While she was living as a student on the Nankai campus, she recalls how the Chinese security guards were vigilant, always on the lookout for religious activities in the dormitories of Uyghur students:

> A Uyghur male student from my university was disappeared by the government just because he was openly religious. Two more Uyghur students at a nearby textile university were detained from their dormitories because they kept the *Qur'an* in their rooms. They disappeared as well. We Uyghur girls had

our own separate dorm, but we shared the bathroom with Chinese students. There was no possibility to practice prayer. You could not perform ablutions in the public bathroom, and there was no room in our dorm to kneel and pray. Besides, we had to be careful. The Chinese are like the Russians, they make people spy on each other. After my friend Yusuf was arrested, the police asked me if I had talked to him. I said no, because if you admit "yes," you will be arrested also.

As a student Arzu was bold in denouncing the oppression of her people. She told her professor she did not want to attend his history class, because it would remind her of the sad reality that Chinese immigrants were given freely the land belonging to the local Uyghurs by the government and the original owners were given very little monetary compensation. She told him her family's story, of how the government had appropriated their farm and given it to Chinese settlers who built a greenhouse on it. She told her professor: "The government gave us very little compensation in return. For 11 acres we received 10,000 yuen—almost nothing!"

Her professor appeared shocked to hear how little money Arzu's family received. He allowed her to skip his classes, only asking her to attend the final exam. Arzu reflects, "I can't believe what I did, given the political situation. I feel so lucky that my professor did not tell the government on me!"

Tensions in the Workplace

Arzu Gul received her bachelor's degree in business administration from Nankai University, Nanjing in 1999. She returned to Korla, having graduated with top marks from one of China's most prestigious universities. She tried to find a job in her home city, but the management in all of the companies she approached told her they only hired Han Chinese graduates. At that time, the local government would assign recent graduates to the "tough governmental jobs" if they could not secure jobs themselves. Thus, after failing to find a job, despite her excellent qualifications, Arzu was sent to a remote village for "training." She was paid a low salary to attend daily indoctrination classes on communist ideology and PRC patriotism. She traveled for at least two hours every day by car to reach that village from her home.

The next year, in 2000, the local government assigned her a job as a translator. Political studies now occupied more than 70 percent of her work time. She had to translate every word spoken by her Chinese supervisor to the Uyghur villagers who gathered at the factory for political study sessions. She describes the indoctrination procedure as follows:

> The important message they would repeat all the time was, "Xinjiang has always been part of China." This is so stupid. Why wouldn't we say, "Beijing has always been part of China?" The government was revealing the truth through their own propaganda.

While working for the government, Arzu was obliged to perform in a Uyghur folk dance troupe that was training for government competitions and danced on the streets:

> The purpose was to create a fake happy mood of Uyghurs. Our instructor was not even Uyghur, she was Mongol. She introduced some Mongol dance moves, so our traditional way of dancing was distorted. The government didn't want us to keep our pure tradition of dance—or why else would they choose her? They just wanted to show tourists and other people that we were "happy Uyghurs" singing and dancing in the street. So, part of my job was to be a forced dancer. I felt very uncomfortable because in Islam we have an ethical rule—to keep a distance between women and men who do not belong to the same family. And when I was forced to dance like this, to hold hands with men, it was hard! I grew up in a Muslim family with four brothers and I was taught what to wear, what to do, therefore it was very difficult for me to be forced to dance with male colleagues in an open public area in the hot sunlight. It was torture for me, especially when they told me to "smile"!

In the early 2000s, Arzu managed to leave China with her husband whom she had known since the sixth grade. After graduating from university in 1999, the couple wanted to get married, but Arzu's mother was ill, so they waited until July 2001. Her husband was destined to become a distinguished international scholar who received scholarships for postgraduate studies, first at Gothenburg University in Sweden and later at the University of Glenmorgan in Wales. This allowed Arzu to leave China and join her husband in Sweden in 2002. In 2008 Arzu and her husband arrived in Canada as skilled immigrants. Her husband worked at Carleton University in Ottawa and today they live in British Columbia with their three children.

The Turning Point: News of Xinjiang's Re-education Camps

In August 2017, Arzu Gul read an article about the mass detention of more than 1 million Uyghurs in Xinjiang's "re-education" camps. "This touched my heart. I could not enjoy my ordinary life anymore; I felt I should speak out."

But Arzu had already "been feeling the oppression of my people in East Turkestan," ever since the last time she visited them in 2006:

When I landed in Beijing Airport my phone suddenly stopped working. When I arrived in my hometown, friends warned me that the police could listen to us, even in our own homes, so I should not be speaking about politics, even with family members. I was followed in the streets as I walked with my relatives. I could not pray in our best friend's house, for fear of causing trouble. While on my way back to the U.K., I was waylaid and almost robbed by a group of strangers in Beijing airport who tried to steal my suitcase.

Arzu spoke of how her family members in Korla have been constantly harassed by police simply because she lives in the West. Although she has lost all contact with them since 2017, she is certain the harassment has escalated. Thus, when she found out about the re-education camps, it was a major turning point: "I realized I must break my silence to become the voice of those Uyghurs who are deprived of their freedom!"

Arzu Gul first started to get involved in Uyghur advocacy work by attending conferences, participating in protests, distributing flyers and "talking to other people, especially Muslims." Later, she began to organize events, collaborating with local Islamic organizations. In March 2018 she organized a major conference, "China's Cultural and Physical Genocide of Uyghurs," at the Anatolia Islamic Centre in Toronto. She recalls that, "At that time no one was talking about Uyghur Genocide; most people still did not know the Uyghurs."

Arzu Gul has approached Canadian politicians and the Canadian Council of Imams, to raise awareness about the Uyghur issue at both the community and government level. In 2019, she began to send letters to Canadian MPs about the plight of the Uyghurs, and she founded the Canadian Uyghur Learning Centre in Toronto to educate Uyghur women and children in Uyghur language and culture. She also co-founded the Darman Foundation to raise awareness about the Uyghur refugee crisis.

Currently, Arzu is part of a team of Muslims, Jews, Christians, and Falun Gong practitioners who seek to raise awareness about human organ harvesting in China, which they claim is a lucrative business that predominantly targets Uyghur and Falun Gong prisoners and is supported by state-sponsored Chinese doctors and hospitals.[xxvi] Arzu argues, "It is a very difficult process, as the Chinese government is strictly controlling the information about this issue."

She also highlights the correlation between the "Halal organ scandal" and the harvesting reports of Uyghurs and other ethnic minorities. According to Arzu, many rich people in the Middle East are buying the so-called "Halal" organs supplied by Chinese hospitals connected to the CCP.[xxvii] She declares, "It is very likely these organs are harvested from Uyghur detainees." She pointed to a photograph of the hospitals near the detention camps and the new airports that are being built around East Turkestan.[xxviii] According to Arzu, "Muslim patients from the Middle East do not know that the Halal organs are being extracted from living persons. If they knew it, they would never want to have the transplant surgeries. In Islam, killing a person is equal to killing all of humanity."

Arzu Gul's Children

The sudden realization in 2017 that her children could no longer speak to their grandparents on WeChat was a major factor in galvanizing Arzu to work in human rights. She notes that some days when she is very busy with her activism work, her daughter and son help her with cooking. "I don't want the stress of my work to affect my family. I try not to shed tears in front of my children. I want my kids to know about the injustices we are facing, but I don't want them to grow up feeling victimized; I want them to be strong. I want them to be able to help our people and anyone else who is oppressed in the world!"

Arzu describes herself as "the luckiest woman in the world" in having a husband who supports her wholeheartedly in her advocacy work.

6. Raziya Mahmut

Interviewed on January 31, 2021

Raziya Mahmut is a prominent human rights activist and advocate for the Uyghur community in Canada. She was born in Ghulja, East Turkestan. She left China on a student visa and moved to Canada with her family in 2007, where she currently resides in Gatineau, on the outskirts of Ottawa. Raziya Mahmut is actively involved in various organizations and initiatives that focus on raising awareness about the Uyghur situation and supporting Uyghurs both within Canada and globally. She serves as the communications director at the Uyghur Academy of Canada (UAC), dedicated to promoting Uyghur culture, language, and rights in Canada. She is also a board member of the East Turkestan Association of Canada and a member of the International Support for Uyghurs (ISU), a Montreal-based nonprofit organization that supports the Uyghurs and other oppressed Turkic peoples in East Turkestan. Raziya is a member of the World Uyghur Congress (WUC), an

Figure 6 Raziya Mahmut. Photographer: Kewser Kamil.

NGO based in Munich, Germany, an international organization of exiled Uyghur groups whose mission is to "represent the collective interest of the Uyghur people." Raziya completed her Bachelor of Science degree in Biology from Shanghai Eastern Normal University in 1993. She furthered her studies by obtaining a Masters in Molecular Biology from Mons University in Belgium in 2006. In 2010, she earned her second Masters in Veterinary Science from the University of Montreal. Her academic journey culminated in 2017 when she received her doctorate (Ph.D.) degree in Biology from Carleton University in Ottawa.

Childhood and Family

Raziya Mahmut was born in 1971 into an intellectual family in the city of Ghulja during the Cultural Revolution. As a child, she gradually became aware of the social inequalities Uyghurs faced. Her older sisters spoke Mandarin at home since they were *minkaohan*[xxix] students attending Chinese schools. Raziya felt there was an emotional distance between them and the other family members (who spoke only Uyghur) and she noticed frequent misunderstandings within her family due to this language barrier. Raziya quickly taught herself Mandarin so that she could communicate with her sisters. She decided to go to a Uyghur school when she reached school age, hoping to avoid a similar alienation from her parents. But her father insisted she attend a Chinese school, arguing that she would not find a job otherwise.

When Raziya was in grade six, there was a "Strike Hard Campaign" in which many young Uyghur men were arrested and sent to prison.[xxx] As she recalls, no Chinese men were apprehended by the police. Thus, Raziya's childhood years were filled with worry and anxiety over news that the police were actively targeting Uyghur people.

Tensions in University Studies

On her first day in the Biology program at Shanghai University, Raziya realized she was the only Uyghur student in the classroom. She recalls how one of her professors challenged her qualification in front of her classmates, saying, "How did you get into this degree? I did not know your school was good enough." Raziya recounts her reaction to the event: "I could not believe such words were coming from a university professor. He made me feel [like] I did not deserve to be in a class at a famous university in Shanghai!"[xxxi]

Raziya felt targeted on campus because she looked different and spoke a different language. When "bad things" happened in the dormitory her Chinese roommates would always blame her. When she went to shop in the local mall, the security officers would spot her and warn the public through their loudspeakers, blaring out, "Xinjiang people are present, so everybody should watch out for their purses and handbags and be extra careful!" She faced similar incidents in other shopping malls and on city buses.[xxxii]

Tension in the Workplace

After graduating from Shanghai University, Raziya found it impossible, as a Uyghur, to find a job in Shanghai. She returned to East Turkestan, where the Minister of Education, a Han Chinese, informed her that it would be very hard for her to find a job because of her ethnicity. She was unemployed for a whole year before she relied on her "connections" (bribes or other illicit approaches) to find a job in a medical college as an assistant lecturer. "It was a big blow to my self-confidence, after graduating with top marks from a top university in China."[xxxiii]

The First Turning Point: The Ghulja Incident

In 1997 Raziya witnessed the Ghulja Incident (also known as the "Ghulja Massacre").[xxxiv] For three days her family could not leave the house because of curfew restrictions. According to her estimate, in the days following the demonstration, more than 60 percent of young Uyghur men in Ghulja were arrested and sent to prison. She recalls that, before the incident, many young Uyghur male university graduates, including her own classmates, operated small businesses. They were not able to find jobs, so that was their only means of livelihood:

> In a big mall, 95 percent of shop owners had been young Uyghur men. A few weeks after the incident, I went back to that shopping center, and found that 90 percent of those men had disappeared. I was told they had been arrested because of the Ghulja incident.

She estimates that between 10,000 and 20,000 people had "disappeared" during that year, 1997. Raziya explained the situation as "collective punishment," which was a common practice in those years. After that incident, political pressure on Uyghurs increased dramatically in her home city. She had to spend long hours in political study sessions at her college. For her, this was a turning point:

> The Ghulja massacre made a big change in my life, so at that time I decided to leave the country. [But]the first time I began to think about finding freedom in the West was in the 1990s, when Chinese immigrants from eastern Chinese territories began flooding into Ghulja.

Raziya recollects that the native Uyghurs were puzzled when they realized that many of the tall oak trees that lined the streets had been cut down in their neighborhoods. Raziya's only Western friend, an English professor at a university in Ghulja, asked her if she knew who had permitted such a large scale cutting of oak trees. Raziya replied that no one had been told the reason. Then her friend observed that in the U.S. and in the U.K. nobody is permitted to cut down trees without the permission of the local residents. This surprised Raziya:

> I was filled with admiration towards the people of the Western countries, where democracy was guaranteed. My Western friends became my teachers on Western democracy and liberalism, so different from the authoritarianism I found in China.

The Second Turning Point: Government Intimidation

In 2002 Raziya left China to study in Belgium. When she arrived in Beijing, traveling en route to Belgium, she was refused by all the hotels, because she was from Xinjiang and an ethnic Uyghur.[xxxv] "I was a homeless person in Beijing, until I could find Uyghur people to host us."

While in Belgium, she applied for Chinese passports for her husband and daughter so they could join her, but her application was refused repeatedly by the Chinese Embassy for four years. Every year, when visiting her family in Ghulja, she was interrogated by the police. Once, she was even dragged into a car with dark windows and brought to an unknown place and interrogated for two hours.

In 2017 Raziya returned to East Turkestan to visit her father who was very ill, but before leaving she was intimidated by the Chinese Embassy in Ottawa and kept under police surveillance. It took three months to get a visa. Finally, she left in May 2017.

She was only allowed to stay for five days, and while she was there, she was surprised to see that the streets and markets were totally empty. "I kept hearing these phrases: 'Everyone is gone,' 'All have been arrested,' or 'We are separated.' They were all too common. My whole country was under high police surveillance and had become a totalitarian state!" Raziya recalled how, when she arrived in Beijing, she was worried she had made the wrong decision [to come to China]: "The man sitting next to me at the airport talked about the Uyghurs. He told me there was an order from Beijing that went, 'If one Uyghur is disloyal to the Chinese Communist Party, then he and all his descendants will be punished until the third generation.' This scared me."

Raziya noticed the police were stalking her as she visited her relatives:

> Security agents followed me, a police car was parked outside the house I was staying in from the very first day I arrived until the day I left, and a policeman followed me to airport to make sure I got on the plane. That was the situation when I went back in 2017. I couldn't help noticing all the police checkpoints and metal detection doors everywhere, and the stores were closing early. They used to stay open until late. I thought it was maybe because after the 2009 Urumqi incident, they put the metal detectors in place, but I didn't realize there was a lot more to it than that. It was crazy to see my family just continue on living, as if life were completely normal. They would tell me, "Oh yeah, we just have to seal our bag to go to the grocery store, and we can't bring any water bottles"—as if this were perfectly normal! I thought, "This is crazy!"

Raziya spoke of her daughter's experience when she visited China in 2016:

> One of her aunts brought her to this big plaza, where there was music and said to her, "Come, we're going to dance here, they have Uyghur music!" But she didn't see any Uyghur people, and there were only Han Chinese people dancing to the Uyghur music. I told my daughter, "That's because the Uyghurs are in concentration camps and Chinese people have replaced us to dance our dances."

Raziya told another story about how the Han Chinese were appropriating Uyghur traditional dress:

> When I was in the airport, there were four ladies, all wearing Uyghurs dress, *atlas,* with the traditional hats. They were typical Han Chinese, speaking in Chinese, and they were on the same plane as me. I was looking at them, thinking, "What are they doing?" They didn't look like artists, actors, but they were dressed up because this plane was going to Urumqi, right, so they were trying out our Uyghur customs, *atlas,* our traditional dress, and *doppa* on their heads. And people were looking at them saying, "Oh these dresses are so perfect!" I was not wearing *atlas,* I was dressed like this. When you consider that many of our people have been arrested for wearing *doppa* or a veil ... that they have been put in prison. So, the Chinese appropriate our culture but punish the Uyghurs who practice their own culture. When I saw them, I said, "Oh ... the dress looks so beautiful!" I was so jealous, I wanted to dress up like this. I tried to buy those dresses at the airport boutique, but my sisters said, "No, we can't buy those things because it is too dangerous, if they find it in your bag in the airport, they might arrest you."[xxxvi]

Immigration to Canada

In 2006 Raziya was able to unite with her husband and daughter in Belgium, and they immigrated to Canada in 2007. But by the end of 2016, she had lost touch with all her relatives in China. She suddenly realized that all her family members and friends back home in China had blocked her on WeChat. The last message she heard was, "Sorry, we should block you."[xxxvii] Three years later, in November 2019, she received a brief message from her sister informing her that their father had just passed away. She notes bitterly: "Death announcements are the only kind of communications that most Uyghurs receive from China these days; there is no normal, everyday means of contact."

Raziya spoke about how the experience of separation from loved ones was a recurring pattern in her family history:

> Separating parents from their children and separating spouses from each other were commonplace in the early years of the Peoples' Republic of China. It happened to my family too. Right after my older [siblings] were born in the early 1950s, the CCP exiled my father to a remote mountain-forest village named Qaraköl, accusing him of being a "revisionist" and later a "counter-revolutionary." It took him two days to travel back home to see his family. He spent years alone in that village before my mother came to his side, leaving all three children to the grandparents.
>
> My older siblings grew up assuming that our grandparents were our parents, and that our birth parents were their big brother and sister. They would call our grandparents "mom" and "dad." Then, my parents were transferred to Monghulküre, far away from where my grandparents lived. Then, my three older siblings left our grandparents to live with our parents.
>
> As a result of more than ten years of separation ... there were daily miscommunications and misunderstandings. After I and my three younger siblings were born, it was natural that my parents paid more attention to us than to their older children, who had been brought up by grandparents. Thus, my older siblings would complain about unequal treatment and show anger towards our parents, even though they knew they did not abandon them on purpose. It was still very difficult to wipe away such tensions in our family. I think this reality left permanent and lifelong pain and trauma in my parents' and older siblings' lives, along with their own children's lives. Similar stories can be found in my husband's family. Intergenerational trauma and family separation are still ongoing in China. Parents are arbitrarily detained in concentration camps or forced labour camps while children are being put into state-run orphanages and indoctrinated in schools outside of East Turkestan.

Life in Canada

Today, Raziya lives with her family in Ottawa and works as a biologist for Health Canada while keeping up with her advocacy work. She speaks Mandarin, French, English, and various Turkic languages. Raziya was apolitical until 2017 because she was worried about the possible impact on family members back home, although, "in my heart, I was always supporting the Uyghur activists who were fighting for the Uyghur cause."

But everything changed in 2017 when she read the first reports on the "re-education" camps in Xinjiang:

> The re-education camps issue pushed my last limit! There is no free media that can cover what is really happening in East Turkestan, so the Uyghur situation might be worse than what happened to the Jewish people in World War II. We are just seeing the surface.

That same year, Raziya reached out to professors at Carleton University to help her organize events on Uyghur issues. She gave presentations at different universities in Montreal and Ottawa and has collaborated with other Uyghur activists in organizing events. She has attended almost all Uyghur-related protest demonstrations in Montreal and Ottawa over the last four years and has published stories and perspectives on the Uyghur issue.[xxxviii]

In her public speeches, Raziya highlights the trauma that Uyghurs in the diaspora are facing as their family members and friends disappear into re-education camps of Xinjiang. Raziya told us in her interview that she has recently been depressed, that sad music can make her cry very easily, and that she often sheds tears when she gives public presentations on the plight of the Uyghurs.[xxxix] She comments:

> People in Belgium and Canada are living their lives 100 percent differently than we are. Westerners are living in Paradise and [the Uyghurs in China] are living in Hell—they just don't know it. If the Uyghurs knew this reality, their dissent would become much stronger. This why the Chinese government is trying very hard to prevent the free flow of information.

Raziya insists that the "Uyghur issue" is a global issue: "Chinese imperialism has already influenced the whole world. The CCP has expanded its dictatorship to Hong Kong[xl] and is now trying to expand its control and authority internationally, through the Belt and Road Project."[xli] But Raziya has found many Canadian universities are reluctant to offer venues for events on Uyghur issues because they fear offending the CCP. She notes, "Their Chinese students represent a major source of income for these universities, and this situation is eroding freedom of speech in Canada." She also claimed that Canadians do not realize how the Chinese view them:

> Nationalism and imperialism do not accept any diversity. Chinese chauvinistic nationalism has been deeply ingrained into the Chinese mindset. This nationalism makes the Chinese feel proud of themselves, while regarding others as backward, under-developed and barbaric. I have often heard Chinese, who are government

scientists, saying that Canadians have only had two hundred years of history; therefore, Canadians are still "primitive people."

Raziya's Daughter

Raziya's daughter, Kewser, was born in East Turkestan, but left her Homeland at the age of 8 with her father to join her mother in Belgium. Raziya tells the story of how, after the family moved to Ottawa and Kewser had been enrolled in a Canadian Elementary school, one day she came home crying.

> She was in Grade 3, and on that day the children had been asked to give a short presentation on their country of origin, but Kewser could not find East Turkestan on the map. She felt humiliated. We, her parents, explained to her how their Homeland was occupied by China, and that was why it was not on the map.

After her mother became involved in Uyghur advocacy work, her daughter Kewser switched her university major from Biology to International Human Rights and Relationship.

Since 2020, Kewser Kamil has been working as a volunteer for International Support for Uyghurs, preparing newsletters for Canadian MPs and organizing and hosting online events. She also works as a volunteer researcher for the East Turkestan Information Centre, with the prominent Uyghur activist, Rukiye Turdush. Since October 2021, Kewser has served as director of the human rights committee for World Uyghur Congress (WUC).

Raziya tells the story of how, in 2019, the CBC/Radio Canada came to their home to interview her. Kewser participated in the interview and became emotional while speaking to the reporters. Raziya commented, "for the first time I felt the heaviness of the burden I had put on my daughter's shoulders."

7. Gulchehra Hoja

Interviewed on May 1, 2021

Gulchehra Hoja was born in Ürümqi, the Capital of East Turkestan. Today she is a distinguished Uyghur American journalist, television producer, and webcaster with over twenty-five years of professional record and experience. She joined Radio Free Asia (RFA) in 2001 and her work involves research, preparing and delivering stories on various issues (Human Rights, Health, Economy, Education,

Figure 7 Gulchehra Hoja. Photographer: Gulchehra Hoja.

Agriculture, and Social Justice) related to the Uyghur people. Many of her reports have been translated into English and published in RFA's press releases.

Gulchehra Hoja is the Winner of the 2019 Sergei Magnitsky Outstanding Human Rights activist awards, and also the Winner of the 2020 International Women's Media Foundation's Courage in Journalism Awards. She was also selected for the list of the 2020 Edition of The 500 Most Influential Muslims. She has also won awards with her colleagues at RFA, such as Tehe Gracie Awards for the RFA's multimedia team's project "Half the Xinjiang Sky" in 2010, and The USAGM Burke Awards in 2019.

Gulchehra Hoja has often shared her own story, at the 2018 U.S. Congressional Hearing, and on May 15, 2019 at "The Dangers of Reporting on Human Rights" U.S. House of Representatives Committee on Foreign Affairs Subcommittee on Africa, Global Health, Global Human Rights, and international organizations. She spoke at the Women in the World Summit in New York on April 11, 2019 and at the Oslo Freedom Forum in 2020.

> *On March 27, 2019, Gulchehra Hoja met with the U.S. Secretary of State*
> *Michael Pompeo as a representative of persons with family members held in the*
> *Xinjiang internment camps. Today, she is a U.S. citizen, and lives near Washington,*
> *D.C. with her husband and three children. Gulchehra Hoja's memoir, "A Stone Is*
> *Most Precious Where it Belongs: A Memoir of Uyghur Exile, Hope, and Survival",*
> *was published in February 2023 by Hachette Books.*

Childhood and Family

Gulchehra Hoja was born on June 17, 1973, in Ürümqi, the capital of East Turkestan/Xinjiang. Her father, Abduqeyum Hoja, was a well-known archaeologist and published historian. Her mother, Qimangul Zikri, was a pharmacist and professor of pharmacology at Xinjiang University. Gulchehra's name means "face of a flower." Her last name means "teacher."

Gulchehra's grandfather, Zikri Elpetta, was a well-known composer who wrote about the Uyghur *Muqam* and musical forms and established a Uyghur arts-and-culture center. Since her parents were hard-working professionals, Gulchehra and her younger brother Kaisar were raised primarily by their grandparents. They grew up in a relatively liberal social environment since Mao's Cultural Revolution came to an end in 1976. The Uyghur schools were staffed by Uyghur teachers who taught in the Uyghur language. She recalls growing up around musicians, dancers, and poets, and dancing at her parents' parties. In 1992, at age 19, she traveled to Japan, to participate in a student dance festival and won a gold medal.

Gulchehra studied at Xinjiang Normal University. Shortly after graduating with a B.A. in Uyghur language and literature, she was chosen to be the hostess for a popular children's program in the Uyghur language on Xinjiang television. She also worked for China Central Television (in Chinese) and appeared in music videos, commercials, and movies. Unlike the other women in this study, Gulchehra had immediate success in her career choice, encountering no apparent discrimination in the job market:

> I began my career at the Xinjiang TV, produced and hosted a variety of TV programs in Uyghur and Chinese language.
>
> I was nationally recognized as the "Class A Anchor" by China's Radio and TV Bureau.
>
> I created a TV program for children in Urumqi, I worked as a television hostess for five years. The program was very successful. I felt I had the children's trust, and I believed the CCP's harsh policies towards the Uyghurs would change.

Gulchehra Hoja soon became a household name in East Turkestan, beloved by her viewers for her charm and rapport with the children on her show. However, this positive situation did not last. Gulchehra described in our interview the events that prompted her to leave China:

> In 2000 the CCP put pressure on us (the TV station) to promote "bilingual education." The idea was that the Han language is best for your children's future. I noticed a policy aimed at our [Uyghur] children, towards our next generation. When I was a child in school there was still the opportunity for a full Uyghur education. I would speak Uyghur in school, and I was surrounded by Uyghurs. But now they started the "bilingual education program" where only Chinese was taught and spoken in middle school.

In the 1990s Gulchehra Hoja had witnessed a steep rise in the Han population in East Turkestan, due to the "Open Far West Policy." She commented, "So, it seemed they changed the educational system in order to force the children to assimilate. I was inside [China], so I could not express my concerns. There was enormous political pressure. I felt very uncomfortable."

In 2000, the Chinese Communist Party established the Xinjiang Class (*Xinjiang neidi gaozhong ban*), a program that funded middle school-aged students from Xinjiang (mostly ethnic Uyghurs) to attend school in predominately Han-populated cities located throughout eastern China.[xlii] Gulchehra explained:

> This meant that gifted children would be chosen from poor families in villages in East Turkestan and flown to Beijing where they were awarded scholarships to live in boarding schools and receive a top education—in the Chinese language. It was presented as a great honour and an opportunity for your child. We had to promote it on our TV shows: "The Xinjiang Ban is here for your Life Future! Please join the Xinjiang Ban!"[xliii]

Gulchehra described her misgivings at the time:

> I saw, I experienced this. I felt I was lying to the parents when I would say it was a great opportunity to study in the big cities. These children were not happy! It was like a "re-education" camp for children. They brainwashed them, they assimilated them, they changed them! Those kids were so confused! They missed their parents. They were forbidden to speak Uyghur. Once a month I would talk to parents who lost their kids, and I would try to convince them of their child's bright future. Most of them hardly saw or spoke to their kids, since it is three and a half hours to fly from Urumqi to Beijing, and these were poor villagers, they couldn't afford it. They would say, "but we are Muslim, we have a different language, different food—it will be so difficult for our children!" My job was to interview the kids on

my show and show the parents how successful they were—but they looked so lost. Many were crying, and they were afraid to speak to me in the Uyghur language, terrified they would be punished. These children were hurting, I could tell. I know children. Children always express their pure feelings. All these happy Uyghur children had become something else. They had become slaves.

In July 2001 Gulchehra was presented with the opportunity to attend a conference in Austria. This was the first time she had traveled to Europe. When she checked into her hotel, she was excited to find the open internet there:

> For the first time, I had a chance to find out what was happening in the Uyghur region. They were pushing us to promote the Han Chinese influence, children were learning Chinese language in primary school, in kindergarten. So, I searched out Radio Free Asia and listened to it every day in my hotel room. It was very different from what I was doing, I realized. I thought, "what I am doing is pure propaganda." I felt I was being used by the CCP. I felt used, guilty. So, I called the RFA management and told them, "I don't want to go back to China. I want to work for Radio Free Asia." They were so happy to hear from me, they hired me on the spot. So, I flew to Washington D.C. and twenty days later I started working for RFA.

After she arrived in Washington, D.C., Gulchehra called her parents to inform them of her decision. After a short pause, her father said, "Oh, my brave daughter!"[xliv] But eventually her decision had negative repercussions on her family back in China, who were questioned by the police: "There were so many problems! They had no passports to come and see me. My parents begged me not to call them again. 'Don't come back!' they warned me. My younger brother was also arrested at this time."

On January 28, 2018, Gulchehra Hoja published her interview with Omurbek Eli, who had been arrested and sent to re-education camp for "terrorist activities" while visiting his parents in Xinjiang.[xlv] This was the very first report of a camp survivor to appear in the media. Three days later, on January 31, twenty-five members of Gulchehra's family were summoned to local police stations in Xinjiang and detained.

Gulchehra described her reaction: "I felt frozen, angry. I was helpless, I didn't know what to do. This was the most difficult time in my whole life. But I chose not to be silent."

In July 2018 she testified before U.S. Congress and gave interviews to the media, hoping to rally support for her family. By doing this, she was setting an example for other Uyghurs, who began sharing stories of their own missing relatives.

After I reported to the U.S. government, they released my mum and I learned that a few of my cousins and my aunts had also been arrested. They were all part of the same WeChat group. I had not spoken to them since 2016, when I was invited to talk to my Uyghur relatives via WeChat.

Gulchehra's relatives were gradually released. Her mother, Qimangul Hoja, was in a re-education prison for two months and described the camp conditions to her daughter over the phone; how there was a severe shortage of drinking water, and how disgusting the food was. She told her daughter, "You must be doing a good job, because you have made them very angry."[xlvi]

Gulchehra still misses her parents' physical presence: "I just want to be a good girl for my parents. Even one meal, I cannot cook for them!"[xlvii]

Gulchehra first heard about the "re-education" camps in 2014 through *Radio Free Asia*. After her own reports came out, the Chinese government tagged her and all RFA journalists as "enemies of China." In 2017, she was accused of "terrorist activities" and placed on China's Most Wanted list. She interviewed the very first survivors to come out of Xinjiang's detention camps.

I have interviewed sixteen camp survivors, and I learned so much. I was inspired by their courage. They are only a few, but these people have changed the perspective of the world about the genocide, because they have first-hand experience. They break down, but then they have the courage to speak to us, to give important testimonies and bring us attention from the governments of Western countries. They all survived because of dual citizenship, or they were married to a foreigner who helped them escape. Recently, Mihrigul Tursun spoke to the BBC, but she spoke to RFA first. Of course, our reporters cannot go to Xinjiang, but other big international news media like the BBC can. So, we collaborate, share our information, and it really brings so much attention and awareness of the Uyghur genocide. Before 2017, most Uyghurs were afraid of speaking up because it might be putting their family at risk. Right now, every Uyghur has someone close to them, a relative in camp. Now, most Uyghurs have become activists because they want to raise their voice for their nation, and for themselves.

In April 2021, videos were released of Gulchehra's mother and brother in which they claimed to be leading normal, happy lives in China and denied Gulchehra's statements in her RFA reports on Xinjiang. Gulchehra could tell they were under duress and says she didn't care if they claimed she was lying:

I was so happy just to see them alive, I didn't hear what they were saying; I just saw they were alive, and they looked better than I had imagined. It was quite obvious that my brother had recently been in prison. His head was shaved, his hair just starting to grow back. I know him. My brother loves his beautiful hair, he would never cut it. I watch the video many times, I see them reading from the script, hiding their eyes from the camera. It gives me a sense of love, as if they are trying to tell me, "Don't worry, we are all alive, everything will be fine." All my prayers during this holy month are: *Please, Allah, give me a chance to see them again.*

Activism or Journalism?

During our interview, Gulchehra Hoja insisted that she was not an "activist" in any sense. She explained that it is important in her work as a journalist that she does not appear to be partisan. She does not attend demonstrations, unless to report on them. Nevertheless, her research and news reports for Radio Free Asia are widely referred to by human rights groups and Uyghur leaders to support their own advocacy work.

In November 2019, Gulchehra Hoja received the Magnitsky Human Rights Award[xlviii] for her reporting on the plight of the Uyghurs in Xinjiang. In 2020, she received the *Courage in Journalism Award* from the *International Women's Media Foundation* and was listed among *The 500 Most Influential Muslims.*[xlix]

Gulchehra spoke about how the Chinese government was commercializing Uyghur women's hair:

> I spent more than sixteen months bringing up this issue. I interviewed the first female camp survivor Mihrigul Tursun in 2018 September, she gave a testimony about all the women's hair being shaved in the camp. Then I asked five other women former camp detainees about their hair, and they all answered the same: their hair was shaved or cut very short. This alerted us to this massive human hair industry using camp detainees. I started to look for a hair company in Xinjiang, and I noticed this pattern of forced labor and then the hair products that began 2017, and I investigated the wigs on the world market and the supply chain links to those hair companies in the Uyghur region. I shared this information with the Customs and Border Protection and they did further investigation. In the end, thirteen tons of human hair products from China were seized at the US border.[l]

We asked if she saw any solutions to the ongoing genocide. She responded:

> This is unacceptable. I cannot understand what they are trying to do. Kill all the Uyghurs? But even this harsh policy cannot change the Uyghurs. No, we are in the twenty-first century. It is happening right before all our eyes. It's a human issue. The darkest stain of the twenty-first century. Nobody can say, "I don't know about Uyghurs." You can turn a blind eye, but you cannot erase this stain in the

twenty-first century. What can you tell your children when they ask, "When this genocide was happening, what were you doing?"

Finally, in 2021 the U.S. announced that China's treatment of the Uyghurs was a genocide. We are just beginning to hope. The next step is to collaborate with the international community to put pressure on China to stop the genocide.

Uyghurs are suffering, but we can end this oppression that started only four years ago when China thought it could get away with it. Since 2017, with the pain of separation and the trauma of the genocide, it is impossible to live a normal life. The only thing that can help is by raising our voices and speaking out.

Genocide is happening in front of the eyes of the world. My mother always told me, "We can lose everything except our determination, and we must never lose our hope."

We asked her, "What about the next generation?"

I feel there is a new generation who are becoming brave people who are struggling for freedom. However, the Chinese government is doing all they can to assimilate our children … They have had a Chinese education, they were indoctrinated with communist ideals, but they are starting to follow the truth. Freedom comes from inside. Even if you live in a free country if you allow your mind to be controlled by the evil madness that is China, you are not free. Today there are so many young activists, bringing us new ideas. Also, our younger generation are being exposed to the development of new devices, and they have a better idea how to use these as tools to raise awareness, how to develop their activism.

I am so proud of our next generation! There is a special connection between family members. No one can stop that. The CCP's plan is not going to work. They put millions of Uyghurs in their concentration camps, but they cannot change what is in their hearts. They can never become Chinese. I believe in the people's power. You cannot stop the love that is in families.

We asked if her own children were involved in Uyghur advocacy.

I don't pressure my children in this political situation, I want them to grow up naturally, to be happy children. But when they say, "Where's my Grandma? Why can't Grandpa come here?" I have to give them the truth. They know their grandparents love them and miss them. After 2017 I tried so hard to hide my sadness from my kids. One day I was washing dishes—it was just a few days after I learned that my parents were missing. My 7-year-old grabbed me from behind. "Mummy," he said, "did I do something wrong? Please forgive me." "Why do you say that?" I asked. "Because you didn't smile at me for two or three days." I felt very bad.

We asked about her work with Radio Free Asia:

> We who are working in RFA, we are not only reporting; we are sending out a message. We are sending hope and care—that the world is paying attention to you. We let our audience know that they have the right as human beings to speak out. There is the worst situation possible right now in the Uyghur region, and they are powerless right now. But we still hope that they can be empowered by the messages the world sends to them. I am hiding my sadness behind a smile because I want to give them hope. I feel lucky to be where I am today, and I need to empower others to be strong and hopeful and that is why I keep smiling.

8. Dilnur Reyhan

Interviewed in French and Uyghur, February 7, 2021

Figure 8 Dilnur Reyhan. Photographer: Gulbahar Jalilova.

Interpreted by Marie-Ève Melanson and Dilmurat Mahmut

Dilnur Reyhan was born in Ghulja in 1983. She left China in 2004 to study journalism and sociology in France. Reyhan obtained her Ph.D. in Sociology from the Université de Strasbourg, France in 2017, and was a postdoctoral fellow at the Université Libre de Bruxelles. The topic of her dissertation was the role of information and communications technologies in the construction of the Uyghur diaspora. Today, Dilnur Reyhan is an associate member of the research centers of CERMOM (Centre de Recherches Moyen-Orient-Méditerranée) and CETOBAC (Centre d'études turques, ottomanes, balkaniques et centrasiatiques) and teaches Uyghur studies at the Institut National des Langues et Civilisations Orientales (INALCO). Since March 2019, Dr. Reyhan has served as the president and founder of l'Institut ouïghour d'Europe. She is the directrice de publication for the franco-ouïghour magazine, Regard sur les Ouïghour-e-s, France's only bilingual magazine published in Uyghur and French. Her research and publications show a focus on women and gender identity issues and on Uyghur nationalism. Since the completion of her doctorate, Reyhan has used her academic status and skills to raise public awareness of the ongoing genocide against the Uyghurs in China.

Childhood and Family

Dilnur Reyhan was born in 1983 in Ghulja, into what she describes as a non-religious, middle-class family. Her parents did not keep a *Qur'an* at home, and Dilnur grew up in a secular environment. Her father, who passed away during her childhood, was an intellectual with a graduate degree. Her grandparents were wealthy landowners in Ghulja, but they lost all their land during the communist regime.

Dilnur Reyhan attended a Uyghur school in Ghulja, graduating early at the age of 14. She notes in our interview that she encountered few Han Chinese during her childhood and was unaware of any discrimination against the Uyghurs; probably because Ghulja was a predominantly Uyghur city in the 1980s. She observed that Han Chinese mostly occupied the jobs in governmental offices, where children were not welcome: "When a Han Chinese appeared on the street, we children would run outside to see what Chinese people looked like." As a child growing up in Ghulja (the "Rebel City"), Dilnur would often listen to adult discussions between her parents and their friends about Uyghur nationalism.

In 1997, when she was 14 years old, because of her high marks in school she was encouraged to leave her family in Ghulja to continue her studies at a university in Mainland China.

Since her previous education had been in Uyghur, she was required to do two preparatory years at the "university of minorities," reviewing the same topics in Chinese (while also studying English) before she could be admitted to a Chinese university. Her ambition was to study medicine at Shanghai University. However, she was informed that Shanghai University had not admitted any students from ethnic minorities since 1996. This shocked her: "I became aware that, as a Uyghur, I did not have the same opportunities as others in China."

Search for Employment

Once Dilnur had completed her preparatory program, she received a list of universities and programs where she could apply. She was disappointed, since the programs listed (mostly in pedagogy or economics) did not interest her. Besides, the universities listed were not the top universities. The only program she liked was at the School of Telecommunications at Peking University. However, her application was rejected. Dilnur explained, "Since my father had passed away, my family was not in a position to pay the obligatory bribe, so someone else took my place." In the end, she was enrolled in a teacher's training program at Lanzhou University. She graduated from in 2003, at the age of 20 as one of the top students of her class.

Resettlement in the Uyghur region

After graduating from Lanzhou University, Dilnur decided to return to her native region, but not to her hometown, Ghulja. Instead, she moved to the Capital, Urumqi. Urumqi was an attractive city for many Uyghurs who had studied in the big Chinese cities, because it allowed them to avoid the "pressure" of the smaller cities in their region while at the same time feeling at home living in East Turkestan.

For a year, Dilnur looked in vain for employment, encountering overt discrimination against Uyghurs in the hiring process:

> I felt there was a strong discrimination against Uyghurs, it really was at a peak back then. The job fairs and employers were quite openly anti-Uyghur and aimed to hire strictly Han Chinese. I was told directly by some employers that they did not hire Uyghurs. Being a Uyghur was a huge handicap, being a Uyghur woman was a double handicap, and being a Uyghur woman who had been educated

in the Uyghur school system was a triple handicap. While the system in China theoretically worked on the basis of merit, this system applied only to Han Chinese. Not being able to find employment was frustrating for me, because I was one of the top students in my class, and I could see how all my Han Chinese classmates had easily found well-paid, good jobs in various Chinese provinces, while it was impossible for me to find any kind of employment in my native region, simply because of my ethnicity."[li]

Looking back, Dilnur admits it might have been a good thing that she was unable to find a job in her Homeland because in the early 2000s new opportunities were opening up for young Chinese students to study abroad at Western universities. At the time, there was only one agency facilitating this process, so she contacted them, passed all the necessary exams (held in Beijing) and left China to study in France in late 2004.

Academic Career in France

On arriving in France, Dilnur's initial goal was to become a journalist, which would enable her to educate the French people in issues to do with Uyghurs and Chinese colonialism. However, first, she needed to learn to speak French—an arduous process—so she felt she should choose a more "practical" discipline. Initially, she chose Communications, and later Sociology. In 2009, she founded the Uyghur Student Association in France, which organized an annual conference on the topic of Chinese colonialism, which was followed by a Uyghur cultural celebration. Dilnur obtained her Ph.D. in 2017 from the Université de Strasbourg. The topic of her dissertation was the role of information and communications technologies in the construction of the Uyghur diaspora. In 2018, Dilnur embarked on three months of fieldwork in Istanbul for a project on gender studies. There she focused on the role of Uyghur women in Istanbul and in the LGBT community. From 2019 to 2020 she was a postdoctoral fellow at the Université Libre de Bruxelles, where she explored the same topics, but in the European context. Her research was interrupted by the pandemic, but she intends to resume it in the future.

Today, Dr. Reyhan is a Faculty Member at the Institut National des Langues et Civilisations Orientales (INALCO), a research institution affiliated with the Sorbonne in Paris, where she teaches Uyghur language, civilization, and culture.[lii]

Political Engagement

Dilnur Reyhan describes her political engagement as "temporary work" which she feels is required in the current political context, although she would prefer to focus on her career as an academic. She explained in our interview how she became publicly engaged in the Uyghur cause ("it was a whole psychological process").

While she had always criticized Chinese colonialism since her arrival in France in 2004, she used to do so in the academic context only. She had made a rule for herself that she would not become involved in any political or advocacy work involving the media and would keep her work strictly academic.

However, in 2017, after learning about the "re-education" camps and what was happening to Uyghurs in their Homeland, Dilnur started to criticize the Chinese regime in public. From 2017 to 2019, she accepted invitations to speak on French radio and was interviewed by various newspapers. Until 2019, she had avoided appearing on television, where everyone could see her face. But in 2019, she finally accepted a request for a TV interview because she felt that the "experts" who were usually invited to comment on events in the Uyghur region of China—usually "white male sinologists"—were not qualified. They were rarely well-versed in the Uyghur language, history, and culture and they tended to espouse a Chinese perspective on the issue. For example, Dilnur recounts that whenever these "white Frenchmen" were asked to explain the situation in the Uyghur Homeland, they would start by explaining that "there were two terrorist attacks in the region, so this is why China is taking all these measures." She felt this was a gross misrepresentation of the situation and that it was her responsibility to speak up, simply because she was much more qualified and could explain the situation more accurately than these so-called experts: "I feel that my people are counting on me to explain the real situation to France."

Dilnur noted that the TV hosts and journalists would often ignore her academic credentials and introduce her simply, as an "activist," after they had introduced the "white professors" by their correct university titles: "I find it strange that other scholars who do more than strictly academic work and engage in politics (like me) can be invited to speak as 'experts' or 'professors,' while I am labeled as an 'activist'—simply because I happen to be Uyghur."

Reflecting on her childhood, Dilnur said: "I was raised in Ghulja the 'Rebel City,' I grew up listening to ideas on Uyghur nationalism. I was involved in a protest demonstration when I was only 16. So, I had this background. After

I came to France, speaking out against the Chinese government was not such a big change, it was just to take a bigger step."

Family in the Homeland

Dilnur Reyhan's family are still living in the Homeland, and she fears for them: "I am very concerned about their security, but it is also part of my personality to take risks. I realize that my public engagement puts my family at risk, but at the same time I believe that if I don't speak up, it will be those unqualified white men who will do it instead of me, and this will harm the Uyghur cause."

Dilnur recalls how, in the summer of 2020, she was contacted by the Chinese authorities, who threatened to take her family hostage. She reacted aggressively, saying if they dared to touch her family, she was going to mobilize the whole of France against them. She explained that it was quite common for the Chinese authorities to request that Uyghurs in France hand over information on themselves and their spouses, even if they are French citizens (with passports, identity documents, employment records).

France's Relationship with China

Dilnur explained that France has a peculiar relationship with China, mainly because of France's infatuation with communist ideology in the 1970s and 1980s. She notes that France was the first country to recognize Communist China, and that some prominent Chinese communists have stayed in France. In the 1970s and 1980s, there was a passionate interest among the intellectual class and university students in Maoist ideology, which lingers until today in the older generation. Many French people supported China in the past, and feelings about the country are just beginning to change.

> France, like China, is a colonial power. This makes French scholars more likely to think that they do not necessarily need to learn Chinese to understand China, or the Uyghur language to understand Uyghurs. This is why those who are invited by the media to speak as "experts" on the Uyghur issue are never people who understand the Uyghurs, rather they are often specialists in China, or Turkey, or in Terrorism Studies. They rarely have any knowledge of Uyghur history or culture. *Voila!*

When we asked Dilnur if she had been inspired or influenced by other Uyghur women activists, she replied, "No." Then she laughed. "But it's interesting, because when I have interviewed Uyghur women in my research and asked them the same question, they have said, 'You.'"

When we asked her if she considered herself an "activist" she responded decisively:

> I do not like to be called an "activist." I am, and will remain, an academic who is only coming forward to address these issues in China because my people are suffering right now, and I feel it is my duty, as a qualified Uyghur woman, to speak up on their behalf. I have risked my family by openly talking against China, because in France if I don't speak, others—especially white males—will talk about Uyghurs. Every time these "experts" talk, they always start by saying, "Well, there was a series of terrorist attacks, and that's why the Chinese government is taking these measures." They *always* start by that! That's why I came out, to break this misconception. My people need me, that is why I am doing this. There is a Uyghur proverb: "Others' affairs make your hands cold." This means, "Others never know your situation better than you do."

9. Zumrat Dawut

Interviewed in the Uyghur language on March 14, 2021

Figure 9 Zumrat Dawat. Photographer: Kuzzat Altay.

Interpretation by Dilmurat Mahmut, translation by Abdulmuqtedir Udun

Zumrat Dawut was born in Urumqi. Today she is a famous camp survivor and whistleblower who escaped from China in 2019 and has since spoken before the United Nations General Assembly in New York in front of ambassadors from twenty-eight countries. Former U.S. Secretary of State, Mike Pompeo, has subsequently cited Zumrat's story in his speeches. Zumrat Dawut has given more than a hundred interviews to the media, politicians, and human rights groups, speaking of the events she witnessed in China since 2009. Zumrat and her family live in the state of Virginia and have sought asylum in the U.S.A.

Childhood and Family

Zumrat Dawut was born in 1982 in Urumqi, the Capital city of East Turkestan. Her father worked in gold mine in Chochek City for ten years, and then worked as a sheep farmer. He had a high school education and his wife left school after sixth grade, as was normal at the time. Zumrat's parents had six children and she was the youngest. Zumrat's father was a devout Muslim and built the mosque in the family's neighborhood.

Zumrat attended a local Uyghur elementary school and later enrolled in Urumqi Art College where she studied dance. But she chose not to pursue a career as a dancer, nor did she work in a government office. Instead, she married a Pakistani man and assisted him in running his business.

Zumrat met her future husband, Imran Muhammad, in 2004 on a bus in Urumqi. He spoke to her in Uyghur and they married in 2005 when Zumrat was 23. Zumrat's brothers were opposed to her marriage, but eventually her family accepted her husband "when they saw how he treated me." The couple had three children. Zumrat assisted her husband in managing their import–export company in Urumqi. Zumrat explained, "My husband opened a company under my name to make things easier for the business as I was a Chinese citizen. We later started importing goods from Pakistan to China. I mainly helped with communication as I speak Chinese fluently."

Becoming an Activist, 2009–16

When asked how and when she decided to become involved in political activism, Zumrat spoke about visiting her husband's family in Pakistan when the Urumqi massacre broke out on July 5, 2009. Soon after she was contacted by Rukiye Turdush, the Canadian Uyghur activist, who asked Zumrat to send her information about the atrocities the Chinese authorities were committing in East Turkestan in the aftermath of the Urumqi Incident.

So, in 2009 Zumrat started to smuggle sensitive news out of China through her husband's Pakistani friends and business partners who would transport documents and photographs to Pakistan which would end up in the hands of the Canada-based activist, Rukiye Turdush, who would then hand over the latest news and reports to the international media. This continued until 2016, when international travel became restricted. Zumrat's secret whistleblowing activities were never discovered, although the police questioned her about her contacts in Pakistan during her detention.

Experiences in Detainment

On March 31, 2018, Zumrat received a call from her neighborhood police summoning her to the police station. Since this often happened, Zumrat did not think much of it ("I did not dress up and I wore my house slippers"). But after arriving at the police station, she was detained all night. She was locked into the dreaded tiger chair and interrogated on three issues:

> First, they asked me about money (4,000 yuan—four thousand Chinese Yuan) my husband's friend had transferred into my account. Second, they asked about my call history with Pakistan. Third, they asked questions about my travel history (I had traveled to several countries, it was arranged by a tourism company). Fourth, they wanted to know about the U.S. visa on my passport. In 2016 my husband had obtained U.S. visas for the whole family. The police asked me what my plans were in the USA. They also asked, "Are you in contact with Rebiya Kadeer?" I was also asked if I had had three children because my religion encouraged me to have more children.

The next morning, Zumrat was taken to a hospital where she was X-rayed, fingerprinted, forced to give blood samples, and recorded for voice recognition. In the evening she was brought to a detention camp where she was handcuffed. Her head was covered with a black sack during transportation. Zumrat was able to identify that the camp was located in an area called Beizhan (Northern Train Station) in Urumqi.[liii]

Zumrat described the camp as crowded and filthy. The detainees could not take showers, and Zumrat didn't shower even once during her sixty-two-day detention. The detainees became so dirty that even the guards would cover their noses. The women were given injections every fifteen days and forced to ingest pills that stopped menstruation. Zumrat suspects there were drugs in the steamed bun they were given for breakfast. Women were not supplied with sanitary pads during their menstruation, but eventually most women stopped bleeding because of the drugs. Police came to take young women out of the cells at night. When they returned, they were crying but could not speak of what had happened to them. Women in the camp were divided into three categories. The more religious a woman was, the higher her rank and the worse treatment she faced. One woman that Zumrat knew was placed in the top category because she had tried to go to Saudi Arabia on a pilgrimage to Mecca.

Meanwhile, Zumrat's husband, Imran Muhammad, was lobbying for her release with the Pakistani Embassy in Beijing. The Embassy officials were reluctant to help him at first, but after he spoke to journalists from international media outlets in Beijing like the BBC and the *Washington Post*, they agreed to take up his cause. Soon, the Xinjiang police called Imran, saying they would release his wife if he returned to Xinjiang to fetch her. They even paid his airfare from Beijing to Urumqi. But they made him promise not to speak to any more journalists.

The Flag-raising Ceremony

After sixty-two days in camp, Zumrat was finally released in June 2018. But soon after, she was ordered to attend the flag-raising ceremony every Monday morning. She and the other Uyghur participants were compelled to sing Chinese Communist patriotic songs, to praise the CCP, and to wish President Xi Jinping a long life. Zumrat commented:

> Based on your performance, you were scored on your flag-raising card. There was someone always watching you. You had to smile. No Han Chinese were ever there, everybody was Uyghur. When the Han see the Uyghurs going past, they mock them, "Hurry up, you'll miss the flag-raising!" They find it funny. If you get a score lower than 90, you are taken back to camp again.

Fines for "Illegal Children"

After one of the flag-raising ceremonies, the Uyghurs were told that everyone with three or more children had to stay back. Zumrat was fined 18,400 yuan ($2,600) for having a third "illegal child" (one more than was allowed under the Chinese Family Policy). The women were given receipts for paying the fine, and Zumrat noticed the amount was different for everyone. "The earlier you gave birth, the less the fine. My daughter was born in 2013, so I only paid 18,400 yuan (around $2600 U.S.), but others were crying because the fine was so high. Some people paid 30,000 yuan, or even more than 100,000 yuan."

At the next flag-raising ceremony, Zumrat recalled, they asked all the women to stay behind. All women with three or more children were taken to an office. They were shown a list of 200 names. They were told they all needed a mandatory "birth control procedure." Five women were scheduled for the following week and Zumrat was one of them. Zumrat's husband, who is a devout Muslim, found this unacceptable, the forcible sterilization of his wife. He went to the authorities and begged, but to no avail.

The Sterilization Procedure

Zumrat describes how in October 2018 she was taken to a clinic, hooked up to an IV, and given a general anesthetic. A local doctor later told her she had undergone a tubal ligation; a procedure that uses keyhole surgery to clip, cut or tie a woman's fallopian tubes. There were four beds in the room, with four women. The doctor who did the surgery told her she could go to the local clinic to get painkillers. Zumrat awoke in pain and she noticed that the other women the room were also in pain. She was given a painkiller by injection, and the next day given another injection to prevent infection. Following surgery, the women were discharged from hospital within a day and taken back to their homes by Community Car. Zumrat kept her sterilization certificate and later exhibited it in the USA.

After her sterilization procedure, Zumrat applied to the authorities to get her passport back so she could visit Pakistan with her husband and children. She promised to return to China within one month and was allowed to purchase return tickets (January 31, 2019 to February 27, 2019) and to travel to Pakistan with her family. Once she arrived, she arranged to have all the documents she had sent to friends translated from Mandarin into English, since it was cheaper in Pakistan. She was preparing them as evidence to back up her story when she arrived in the U.S.

Constant Surveillance and Spyware

Zumrat Dawut spoke in our interview about the Chinese state's constant intrusion into the private lives of Uyghur citizens.

After 2016, she told us, the authorities distributed free devices used for television to Uyghur families, who discovered cameras inside the devices that were recording their daily life. "They install recorders in homes also," Zumrat said, "you have to be very careful speaking in the family. There was a bar code on every family home installed behind the main door that collected information about the family, like how many members, their ages. Every few days officials would come by to check it." Also, there were CCTV cameras. Every Uyghur had to install a Spy App on his or her cell phone.

Zumrat described how Uyghurs were under surveillance when they went out shopping:

> The shopkeepers are told to watch their customers. If anyone goes to a restaurant and asks, "Is this a Halal restaurant?" the manager presses a button and the police will come. If anyone buys a knife, the shopkeeper presses a button and the police come to install a bar code. But this happens only to Uyghurs. If you go to a bakery and buy a lot of bread, you will be asked why you buy so much. You are not allowed to stockpile, because you might be hiding someone in your home. So shopping is one way to spy on the Uyghurs. If you go out to get gas in your car, if you get too much they will ask why so much, if too little, you will also be asked. If you don't drive your car for four days, you will be asked why (it's not seen on the cameras). If you stay home for more than three days, you will be asked why you are not going out.

Control over Family Life

Zumrat notes, "As a Uyghur you cannot accept guests any time you like. Even your married daughter cannot visit your home without going to the police for permission. They check the background of every person you are going to visit. If everything is ok, they issue you a letter, and then you can go. Every Saturday the children have to take pictures and send them to the police for identification purposes. The local community distributes free milk for children. It is mandatory—but the Han Chinese would not let their children drink the milk. The Uyghurs were forced to. My husband told the officials that children wouldn't drink the milk so they didn't need to bring milk. However, the officials questioned why we didn't want the milk and told us that this could indicate an ideological issue for us. So we had to accept the milk. As a child we had to have injections given by the local authorities—we feared it might harm us. Abduhelil (my brother) and I always avoided the injection for our children. I never trusted it."

Zumrat noticed that every Friday her children did not want to go to school because plainclothes policemen would come and take the Uyghur children into another room and grill them. They would ask the kids questions like, "Do your parents pray?" and "Do you have a prayer mat? Do your parents teach you the Qur'an?"

> There are many cases of parents taken to the camp because of their children's incriminating answers. That is why the children are so afraid. If they spoke wrong, their mother would be taken away again. Of course, the children notice when their parents are taken away, and because of this they call it "Cursed Friday." Children hate to go to school on Friday. I was able to tell my children about what to say and not say, but it was difficult.

Zumrat added: "Another reason my children did not want to go to school was that Uyghur children were forced to wear Chinese traditional attire at school—something the Han children *never* wore."

Zumrat's son was 12 years old when she saw the picture of him in a historic dress. She noted, "The Chinese have an expression: 'Live like us or die!' You have to become more Chinese than the Chinese to survive."

The "Relatives" Program

The CCP started a new program for the integration and "sinocization" of the Uyghurs. They would assign a Han "relative" to regularly visit and stay at each Uyghur home.

> l had one, and my daughter was 11 years old when she was assigned a 20-year old Han Chinese man as her "relative." He would come to our home to stay over ten days every month. I had to take care of him *very well*, because he would be giving me a score for my hospitality." Zumrat had to prepare his bed ("and in Chinese culture they wash their feet every night"). She had to prepare clean bedsheets and warm water for his feet. "It can happen that the hostess has to wash the relative's feet, but he did not insist. If I did not take very good care of him, I might be taken to camp."

On many occasions, Zumrat told us, the male "relative" (age 20) began to demand that her 11-year-old daughter go with him to his house for an overnight stay. He would call Zumrat late at night, obviously in a drunken state, saying, "Let me take your daughter to my house this night." She would put him off by saying her daughter was sick.

> Once I put a bandage on my daughter's hand and so I was able to refuse his request, but many parents were not able to refuse the male relative's demands. We felt the state encouraged such practices. Very possibly, the authorities planned and encouraged such practices, otherwise he would not dare to do this.

The Whistleblower: Zumrat's *modus operandi*

Once Zumrat had escaped from China, she was able to launch her whistleblowing campaign in the U.S. to expose China's human rights abuses. What made her particularly effective as a whistleblower was the fact that, since the 2009 Urumqi massacre, she had been meticulously collecting documents and photographs, hiding them in her home or smuggling them out of East Turkestan with the help of her husband's Pakistani friends and business associates and had them translated into English in Pakistan ("where it is much cheaper"). Thus, she arrived in the U.S. well prepared, with an arsenal of evidence to back up her claims, ready to speak to the *Washington Post*. Even during our online interview, she kept flashing photographs and sharing documents with our team. She exhibited her notebook where she had recorded the scores on Uyghurs' participation in the flag-raising ceremonies. Zumrat was proactive in her campaign and approached the journalists herself in the beginning.

Zumrat talked about the destruction and desecration of Muslim cemeteries, claiming the Chinese authorities, on deciding to confiscate the cemeteries, would dig up the corpses and contact the next of kin ("We were told, 'just keep them at your home'") [Zumrat showed us a photograph of her mother's skeleton]. "So, many people had to take the bodies from the cemetery and keep them at their home for a month. Muslims do not use coffins, which makes it more difficult." [She displayed photographs of dead bodies exhumed by Chinese officials.]

When Zumrat talked about the flag-raising ceremony she was obliged to attend, she showed us her "report card." As she described her painful, humiliating sterilization procedure, she produced the certificate she had received, as well as the receipt for the fine she paid for having one "illegal child."

She also showed our team her pictures of fake imams in the new fake mosques, set up for "propaganda reasons"; claiming that "all the real imams had been arrested and sent to prison for 10 or 15 years."

She explained her *modus operandi* as follows: "Chinese authorities are afraid; they know they are doing something wrong. That's why, before leaving China, I had documented everything. People do not believe such things could happen in the twenty-first century. I had to bring evidence to prove it."

China's Strategies of Silencing and Reprisals

In September 2019 Zumrat made a speech at a panel discussion of the UN General Assembly in New York before ambassadors from twenty-eight countries. Former U.S. Secretary of State, Mike Pompeo, subsequently cited Zumrat's story in his speeches. Following these events, she reports, the police used her brother, Abduhelil Dawut, to try to silence her.

First, he sent her warning messages: "Don't speak out or do things that harm us."[liv] She disagreed and continued to speak in public. Twelve days later, her father was detained by the police and within two weeks was dead on October 12, 2019. Her Chinese neighbor sent her videos showing people coming to the house next door to pay their respects to her father.

Her brother, Abduhelil, in his interview with *The Global Times*, claimed that his sister had never been to a vocational education and training center, and that "when she delivered her third child, she was found to have fibroids and later had surgery." He also claimed their father had "neither been interrogated nor detained" but had died of heart disease.[lv]

Zumrat's Women Role Models

When we asked Zumrat if she had been inspired by other Uyghur women, she identified Rukiye Turdush, who had asked for her aid in the wake of the Urumqi Incident. Zumrat also heard about Mihrigul Tursun through a practice she had been compelled to participate in while a prisoner in the camp.

> It is called *Criticizing Someone*. They gather people together to learn professional criticism, to criticize China's opponents. In the camps we Uyghurs learned that one of us—a Uyghur—had dared to speak out against the CCP, against China. We were so happy! I thought, "If I ever get to go out of this country, I will speak out just like Mihrigul Tursun!"

Zumrat, however, gives the most credit to her husband: "After arriving in the U.S., my husband encouraged me to speak out. My husband is the person who has influenced my activism the most."

10. Mihrigul Tursun

Interviewed on December 7, 2021 and on February 9, 2022 in English and the Uyghur language.

Interpretation by Dilmurat Mahmut, translation by Abdulmuqtedir Udun.

Mihrigul Tursun is one of the earliest camp survivors who escaped from China in 2018. Her harrowing stories of life inside Chinese prisons and re-education camp have been widely reported in the international media. She testified at the

Figure 10 Mihrigul Tursun. Photographer: Kuzzat Altay.

United Nations and at the Uyghur Tribunal. She has participated in many demonstrations and joined in a three-day protest in front of the White House. She has been interviewed more than 400 times by different news outlets in four languages: Uyghur, Chinese, English, and Arabic. On November 26, 2018, Mihrigul Tursun gave her testimony at the National Press Club in Washington, D.C. On November 28, 2018, she testified before the Congressional-Executive Commission on China. In December 2018, Tursun received a Citizen Power Award. In 2019 a Japanese manga by artist Tomomi Shimizu, told Mihrigul Tursun's story in comics and was a viral hit on the internet. Mihrigul Tursun's autobiography, co-authored with a German journalist, Andrea C. Hoffman, Place of No Return: How I Survived China's Uyghur Camps, was published in March 2023.

Family and Childhood

Mihrigul Tursun was born in 1989 in Cherchen county in (East Turkistan). Her mother passed away in childbirth, so Mihrigul and her two siblings were raised by their father and their stepmother. Mihrigul describes her parents as "Muslims who hid their religious activities." And her father was "very religious and a proud Uyghur nationalist (in a good sense)." Mihrigul's father worked for the Cherchen transport company as a bus driver. "My father had primary school education. At his time, people found jobs after primary school. My father cannot write Uyghur script (the current Arabic script)—he still writes Uyghur in Latin letters."[lvi]

As a child Mihrigul attended a Uyghur language primary school in Cherchen county. She left her parents and her home province at the tender age of 11 to pursue her secondary and university education in Guangzhou in Guangdong province. She explained how the Chinese authorities had sent her to study in Mainland China as part of the new "Xinjiang Ban" policy. Top students were chosen from every city in East Turkistan, based on their marks in an examination.

> The Chinese authorities sent me and other Uyghur students to an inland boarding school in Mainland China. There were 6,000 students in the school, and only twelve Uyghur students among them. There was only one Uyghur allowed in a class. I was the only Uyghur in the dormitory room as well. We had to speak Chinese and wear the same clothes as the Chinese students.
>
> The first year was very hard for us Uyghurs, as our Chinese was not good. Also, we were only allowed to visit our home once a year. In the school it was not easy to meet other Uyghurs, and when we did happen to meet, we had to speak Chinese as we were closely monitored. We studied Chinese Language, Chinese history, mathematics, geography, law. Also, I studied information technology and business administration. Everything was taught in Chinese.

We asked Mihrigul if she had felt lonely being away from her family.

> Of course! It was very hard for us being separated from our family, language and culture. When I first arrived, there were three Uyghur girls in the same school with me, and they killed themselves. Yes, their names were Shiringul, Raziye, and Hushgul. I never knew their family names. In 2000, the second time the Chinese government sent Uyghurs to Mainland China, we had twelve Uyghurs in the school. Every year many Uyghur students committed suicide. It was very hard, we felt a lot of pressure. The teachers also didn't treat us the same as other Chinese students. Even I was beaten by three Chinese girls in the classroom and in my dormitory. It was very hard. So, after two or three years we [Uyghur students] realized it was impossible to live with the Chinese people in peace, although their purpose was to assimilate us. We felt the difference, we realized we cannot mix with them.

Student Life in Egypt

In 2010 Mihrigul graduated from Guangzhou University and applied to study in the U.K. ("I tried to apply anywhere just to get out of China.") She was accepted by a university in London, England. "But the tuition fee was very high. I couldn't afford it, so then I chose a British university in Cairo, Egypt, as it was much cheaper." In December 2010, Mihrigul flew to Egypt on a student visa:

> At first it was good in Egypt. I started by studying Arabic and the first year was language classes. From the second year, we were taught our major. My major was business administration. There were no other Uyghur students, I lived with an Egyptian and a Turkish girl. But three months after I arrived, there was a political problem in Egypt. At that point the Chinese government made us return to China. I spent two months in Urumqi and then I returned to Egypt to continue my studies. Then, three months later, the Chinese government ordered all the Uyghur students to come back to China to update their passports. (This was not required for the Han Chinese students in Egypt.) At this point, my parents told me to not come back, to find a way to stay in Egypt. They were worried that I might not be able to leave China if I came back. There is no guarantee for any Uyghur who is studying overseas to renew his/her passport at the Chinese embassy.

One reason Mihrigul was fearful about returning to China was because she thought she might have a criminal record due to her role in the 2009 Urumqi Incident.

> I was certain that I wouldn't be able to return to Egypt if went to China. I know this 100 percent because I circulated a video on my QQ account during the events of 2009. I was put in jail for eight days in Guangzhou for sharing this video of the Chinese workers killing Uyghur workers in a factory in Shaoguan, Guangzhou, the event that triggered the Uyghur students' protest in Urumqi on July 5, 2009. This was written in my criminal record, and I could be arrested due to this. This was also the reason I first decided to leave China.

When asked to explain her involvement in the Urumqi Incident, this was her story:

> In 2009 I was studying in Guangzhou. My school was very near to the city where the Uyghur workers were attacked and killed. My friend who was living in Shaoguan sent me the video she made from her balcony. I quickly uploaded it to the internet. I didn't think the police could find me so easily.[lvii] I don't know how they knew it was me, but a lot of police came to the campus and took me

away, also a Uyghur male and five or six Chinese students. I was 20 years old at the time. I was very scared, and I realized that I had to leave China. So that's why I applied to a university overseas.

Mihrigul explained how she had married an Egyptian to avoid returning to China, and how her father had disrupted her marriage:

> I first met my future husband, Mahmoud, at the airport in Cairo when I arrived. He helped me find the address of my school and we exchanged our phone numbers. So, the second time the Chinese government phoned, ordering me to return, I asked him to marry me to help me get residence in Egypt. He didn't know anything about the Uyghurs. I explained to him about our culture. We didn't tell our parents and got a marriage certificate. We were married but only on paper. But we Muslims don't accept the paper. We needed to get the parents' permission and do *nikah*. Also, as I was holding a Chinese passport, I needed to get a certificate to prove that I am a Muslim. I went to Al-Azhar University for a three-day class, prayed and got the certificate.

When asked about her feelings for her husband, Mihrigul replied:

> At first, I just thought "I need to marry any Egyptian to get residence." Later, as my husband helped me a lot, I started loving him. He taught me about Islam and many things. If you go to the Egyptian government, they give you *nikah* and a marriage certificate. But we wanted to have a wedding party. We planned everything, the party, the dress. I wanted to have my parents agree to this 100 percent. So, after one year, I invited my parents to come to Egypt—but I didn't tell them I had gotten married to an Arab man. My parents wanted me to marry a Uyghur. When they learned that I had married an Arab, they couldn't accept it. My father told me "I can accept now that you go back to China even if you get jailed, or I will break your legs and keep you at home. I will never allow you to break our lineage!"
>
> My father told me to choose between him and my Arab husband. And I chose my father and left my husband because I cannot find another father.
>
> We were living in Cairo. My husband had bought a home for me. I had my residence visa and I still had two years to complete my degree. But my father wanted to take me back to China. I begged my father to let me finish my degree. I promised him [I would] divorce my Egyptian husband and marry a Uyghur man. So, my father introduced me to his friend's son, Irfan, in Egypt, and then left for China. I stayed back in Egypt because in Islam you have to wait for three months after a divorce to be married again. After we were engaged, Irfan had to return to China as part of the hundreds of other Uyghurs on the Chinese police request. So, I lost contact with him too, but he was never my husband. I don't

want to talk about my Egyptian husband as I don't want to disturb his family in Egypt. So, when I was asked about my personal life in interviews, I only talked about this Uyghur man whom I was supposed to marry but then he left for China and was sentenced to sixteen years in prison.

Mihrigul spoke about her pregnancy and the birth of her triplets:

I was sad to leave my husband, he left for Dubai after our divorce, and we lost contact. But I must not make my father angry. Then, one month later, I knew that I was pregnant. I thought of getting an abortion, but it was illegal in Egypt. I told my parents about this. They told me to give birth to the child. Then, one month later, I learned that I was pregnant with triplets. I wanted to tell my ex-husband, Mahmoud, but I couldn't find him. The hospital required that either my legal husband or my parents sign the surgery papers [for a cesarian birth]. I contacted my former husband's family and they helped contact Mahmoud. He arrived from Dubai, he was engaged to be married again at this time. The doctors told me that the surgery was very dangerous, that my health was not strong enough to give birth to triple babies and that I had a 1 percent chance of survival. I said I had decided to risk the surgery, but I required that my babies must be sent to my parents in China if I don't survive. I made my request in a video, it is still with me now. But the surgery was successful, I didn't die. My babies got their Egyptian passport, I was told that I was able to apply for Egyptian citizenship, but I didn't want to, since I believed the Chinese passport was stronger.

Why Mihrigul Returned to China

Mihrigul explained her reasons for returning to China as follows:

My babies were the first grandchildren in our family. My parents wanted to see them too. I thought, "I will just go, show them the babies, and then come back." I had a return ticket too. I never thought I would not come back for three years! So, I told my former husband to give me two months for me to go to China and show the children to my parents. He agreed and I arrived in China on May 12, 2015. But as soon as I arrived at the Urumqi Airport, I was detained. As I then lost contact with Mahmoud, he tried to get a visa to go to China and find his three children, but it was refused for the next three years. So, he thought I lied to him, took away his children, and blacklisted him from entering China. From 2015 to 2018, he went to the Chinese Embassy more than eighteen times to apply for a visa. His application was refused every time. Hence, he believed I had told the Chinese government to not give him a visa. I was not allowed to leave China or contact him for this period. This started when I was 26 years old.

Three Years in Chinese Camps and Prisons

Mihrigul described the terrible years from 2015 to 2018, when "I never left East Turkestan":

> The first time they released me from prison was because my son Mohannad died. I didn't realize it at the time, but they wanted me to take my other kids from the children's hospital.
>
> I cried when I saw my father who came to get me at the prison. I told him I was sorry I didn't listen to him, couldn't become the girl that he wished me to become, and thus I caused a lot of trouble for them. My father expected a lot from me. So, I think I didn't fulfill my father's expectations. In our tradition, the father is like a king. We respect our father a lot, we keep quiet when he speaks, even after we are married.
>
> My father drove me to a children's hospital in Urumqi. The hospital had put my three children on three different floors, in rooms where I could only see them from behind a glass wall, and they had been given oxygen. But the doctors didn't let me see my son Mohannad. My stepmother cried and asked me to go home and take a rest. We came back the next day and took my son Moez and daughter Elina home. The next day, my father told me that we needed to go to hospital to fetch Mohannad. When we arrived in hospital, I was told that Mohannad had just died. I later learned that Muhaned had died when I was in prison and that is why I was released for a short period. I think I was released as soon as my son died. We buried my son Mohannad in a cemetery in Urumqi.
>
> My brother was in Cherchen at the time. We, as Uyghur Muslims, have the Islamic funeral tradition, we take the deceased to a mosque to pray the Islamic funeral prayer, read *Qur'an*, but the Chinese government didn't allow us to have a proper Islamic funeral, they didn't even allow other people to come to the funeral. Nobody is allowed to cry when somebody dies. For example, my stepmother has two sisters. When their husbands or one of our relatives died, we couldn't visit them to say our condolences or bring food for them.
>
> So only my father, my stepmother and I went to the cemetery to bury my son. My father buried him while my stepmother and I waited in the car. Two police cars were watching us. It was so hard for me as a mother. Then we went back to Cherchen. It was 1,900 km from Urumqi to Cherchen. I stayed with my parents in Cherchen until 2016, for about a year. My father was very excited to see my two babies. He sat with them on his lap, he loved them a lot and even gave them Uyghur names.

When we asked Mihrigul what it was like living in Cherchen with her parents again, she responded, "It was not pleasant, this year I spent with my parents." This was because she was subjected to the "Becoming Family" policy. She described her experience as follows:

From the moment I arrived in China in May 2015, until I got out in April 2018, I was never left alone. When I was at home with my parents, two police officers accompanied me and watched me at home. The only time I was alone was when I went to the washroom. We couldn't pray at home, and when my father wasn't home, my stepmother and I were scared. We knew the Chinese police didn't respect us and we were afraid that they might harm us. Every time I went into the kitchen, the Chinese policeman would try to touch me, kiss me, and hug me. I almost felt that prison was better than being watched at home. I heard that our 37-year-old neighbor committed suicide because her "relative"—the Chinese man at her home—sexually harassed her 8-year-old daughter and the next day tried to rape her. So she killed the Chinese man, her daughter, and then herself. She did so because she knew that she would be given a death sentence for killing the Chinese man and she didn't want her daughter to suffer at the hands of the Chinese. She was our neighbor, her name was Amangul and she was a medical doctor.

My father was there with us at home, but sometimes he had to go out to do shopping. We could not tell him what was happening, we'd just tell him, "Let's call delivery," or "let my stepmother do the shopping." Of course, if I told my father about the sexual harassment, he would kill the policeman. And I don't want to lose my father! Many Uyghur men have committed suicide out of shame. I know in Cherchen more than four Uyghur men committed suicide. A Uyghur man who works at the government threw himself out of the window. He had wife and a daughter. Nobody knows what happened, but I think I know.

Whenever we want to go visit our family members, we need to ask our Chinese "relatives" at our home for permission and give them the details of why and how long we want to visit and get their signature. When we come back, we need to report on what we talked about.

Mihrigul was soon subjected to a second extrajudicial arrest and spent time in prison without knowing the charges against her.

The second time they arrested me was when my two kids became a little better. They claimed that they found new evidence to arrest me on new charges. I was tortured for three days this second time. After that, they took me to a hospital in Urumqi, did medical examinations, and sent me to prison. Within two months, I witnessed nine women die in my cell. Every day three or four women would be taken out, and three or four new women would be taken in. The conditions were very bad, there was no shower, no drinking water, the food is very bad, there is a bad smell, and every week I had to take a strange medicine. On June 9,

Patigul, a woman who was very close to me, died. I cried a lot that day, I was very depressed and passed out.

When I opened my eyes, I was in No. 2 Hospital in Urumqi. When I woke up, I realized I was handcuffed to the bed, and there was a policeman outside watching me. I didn't know how I came to this hospital, it was 1,900 km away from Cherchen! A doctor came in the morning and evening to give me medicine. After taking the medicine, I vomited the medicine in the bathroom. I believed the medicine was something bad. I could not take a shower even in the hospital, because I could only go to the bathroom when the policeman escorted me, so I couldn't take a shower in front of a man.

Mihrigul's Escape from China

Mihrigul told us the suspenseful story of how she escaped from China with her two remaining children, thereby avoiding her own scheduled execution. In this narrative, her former husband, Mahmoud, emerges as a caring father and a courageous and resourceful ally:

> The third time they took me to prison, I was told that they had enough evidence to sentence me to death, and they gave me two months to think about how I can help the Chinese government. I was given three different options to die: by shooting with gun, by killing with medicine, or by giving my body to hospital. If I chose the shooting with gun, I must pay 600 CNY. They asked me to sign a paper to pay this money. I told them, "If you want to shoot me, just shoot me. I don't have money to pay for it. Just choose any option you want."
>
> After one week, they wanted me to sign a paper to give my children to the Chinese government. I rejected it saying that my kids were Egyptian citizens and if they didn't let my kids leave, they would have a problem with Egypt. The police went to my home and took my kids' passports. But the passports had already expired. So, the Cherchen police contacted the Egyptian Embassy in Beijing. Actually, the local police in Cherchen weren't supposed to do this; they didn't have the authority to contact a foreign country's embassy. But the Cherchen police told the Egyptian Ambassador that there are two Egyptian children here and asked them to take the children back to Egypt. But the Ambassador then asked how the children had ended up in Cherchen and contacted my ex-husband Mahmoud. The Embassy asked Mahmoud to come and take his children.
>
> Mahmoud was surprised, because his application for a Chinese visa had already been rejected eighteen times. But in February 2018, Mahmoud, my ex-husband, got a Chinese visa, arrived in China, and came to Cherchen with the Egyptian Ambassador. When he saw the two kids, he asked about his other son and me. So the police came and got me from prison, but first they made me

change clothes and wash my hair and put on make-up. They told me to just sign the papers so that my children could go back to Egypt with their father.

I realized that as soon as my kids left for Egypt, they would be able to execute my death sentence. The police took me from prison to the immigration office, and I saw my husband with the Egyptian Ambassador and more than ten Chinese policemen. We were meeting for the first time after three years. Then the police brought our daughter, Elina, to us. I spoke to my husband in Arabic, as the Chinese police didn't understand Arabic. I told him, "They killed your son, the other two kids weren't with me, I was in prison, and they are going to execute me after one month. I never lied to you, because for the last three years I never had a chance to contact you. Please help me, ask them about your son."

My ex-husband was shocked. A Chinese policeman tried to stop me from speaking and my husband punched him. The police took out their guns, and my husband said, "Come on, shoot me, but you can't shoot because I am not a Chinese citizen." Then the police lowered their guns, and everybody calmed down.

They brought in an English interpreter who talked to Mahmoud for over an hour. But they didn't explain the death of my son Mohannad; instead they lied, claiming I had come to China with only two kids. But I told my husband the truth, everything in English. They told my husband to take the two kids but that he could not take me since I was "a very dangerous woman." The police offered a large bribe to my husband if he would leave me behind. The police also denied any knowledge of my son Mohannad. They did not realize it, but my husband was recording the conversation on his cellphone, so we have proof of what they said.

The police were worried that if I were to get out of China, I would expose the atrocities I had witnessed. I had been inside many prisons and detention camps. My husband didn't accept their offer and insisted he would take me with him. The Egyptian Ambassador was there the whole time and witnessed everything. He told the police that, since my husband was Egyptian, I was eligible to apply for Egyptian citizenship and that the Embassy would approve it right away. Hearing this, I immediately told them I wanted to apply for Egyptian citizenship. I filled out the application, signed the papers, and then told the Chinese police I wished to cancel my Chinese citizenship as Chinese law does not recognize dual citizenship.

On April 5, 2018, after more than three months, I came out of that cell and was able to finally see my kids. I did not see my parents anywhere and was not allowed to ask about their whereabouts. I left my home town three days later with my two children and stayed in Beijing for about twenty days because I was denied from boarding the plane three times for allegedly missing documents. On my fourth attempt, I was able to board on the plane and landed in Cairo on April 28.

Despite her successful escape from China, Mihrigul and her relatives continued
to be harassed by the Chinese authorities.

> So that is how I escaped from China. But because of this, the Chinese police
> took twenty-six of my relatives to concentration camps. The police then told me
> that, after delivering my kids to Egypt, if I would come back to China within two
> months, and if I wouldn't tell anyone what happened, then they would release
> my relatives and give me back my Chinese citizenship. But if I didn't come back
> within two months, they warned me, or if I told anyone what had happened,
> then I would not see my relatives ever again. The police also warned me that
> China had the power to bring me back from anywhere in the world.
>
> Before I left, they made me sign papers saying, "I love China and the
> Communist Party," and that I had been treated well. They also recorded me
> saying all those things on video. After I arrived in the U.S., I tried to persuade
> the Chinese government to release that video, but they didn't. I think they
> understood that no one would believe it. On our way from Beijing to Cairo,
> we had a transit stop in Dubai and my husband got off and stayed back in
> Dubai. His family welcomed me when I arrived in Cairo. My husband told
> me to come to Dubai after getting my Egyptian ID card, as we were worried
> that the Egyptian government was working with the Chinese government and
> might force me to return to China. The Egyptian authorities didn't give me
> the necessary documents right away and then asked me to come to the police
> station. But I didn't go to the police, I didn't trust them. Instead, I hid at my
> husband's relatives' home with my kids. While in hiding, I contacted journalists
> to try to tell the world about what had happened, but nobody would listen to me.
>
> Then, I went to the U.S. Embassy in Cairo to tell them what had happened.
> I wanted to give them my kids in case I got deported back to China. The U.S.
> Ambassador helped me and arranged a hotel for me to stay in. After two months,
> I came to the U.S. with the help of the U.S. Embassy. Then I heard that after I
> escaped to the U.S., the Egyptian government fired the Egyptian Ambassador
> who had helped me get out of China.

Challenges in the USA

Mihrigul said the last time she saw her brother and stepmother was in November
2017, just before she was taken to prison for the third time. She described how
her relatives and her former fiancé were forced to denounce her:

> My brother was a taxi driver, but after I left China, the Chinese government
> made my brother (who never even finished high school) a head of a department

in the police in order to bribe him to stand against me. His Chinese language skills were poor, but when they made him give testimony against me the last time, I realized that they had taught him Chinese, that he speaks good Chinese now. He didn't have the education to become a policeman, so I understand that they wanted to make him fight me.

My stepmother was forced to deny that my baby was killed in the hospital. She had to say it. She has had kidney surgery and every three months she has to undergo blood cleansing. It requires a lot of money and if she is not allowed to travel to Urumqi to do her blood cleansing, then her life will be in danger. My stepmother didn't go to school, she can't even write her own name. But she was afraid of offending the government and ending up being stuck in Cherchen, not able to travel to Urumqi to get her treatment. She can't walk very well and so she uses a wheelchair.

My former fiancé was also forced to speak out against me in a video. After I met with the U.S. Secretary of State, Mike Pompeo in 2019, the Chinese government made him denounce me. His name is Irfan Husen. He said I was a bad girl, that I was sick, and had a contagious disease. Hua Chunying, the spokesperson for the Chinese Foreign Ministry claimed the same thing; that I had a contagious disease and that was the reason I was released from prison after twenty days; to protect the police from contracting the disease from me. In fact, I was in prison for almost three years, but Hua Chunying lied, saying I was detained for twenty days only. That's how I learned that Irfan was detained in China.

We asked Mihrigul what it was like being a camp survivor.

I was one of the first survivors to come out of the concentration camps. While I was in prison, I promised myself that I would tell the world what happened to us if I ever got out alive. When I started speaking about my experiences after I came to the U.S., I received phone calls from Chinese police and my parents asking me to stop talking and accusing me of lying. But I definitely didn't agree with them. Then, the Chinese TV stations broadcast news about me, defaming me. The Chinese government forced Uyghur people to write against me, scold me, and push against me.

When other concentration camp survivors came out of China, they contacted me, people like Zumrat Dawut, Qelbinur Sidiq, Tursunay Ziyawudun. They all said they saw my video while they were in China, and that is how they got to know of me. They saw my testimony to the U.S. Congress and said they were happy in their hearts while they were being forced to denounce me.[lviii] And I have spoken to many news outlets in Taiwan and Hong Kong in the Mandarin language, and this has upset the Chinese government a lot.

Mihrigul described obstacles she has faced in the USA, particularly in applying for refugee status:

> I applied for asylum in the U.S., but I didn't get it yet. My lawyer says that since I hold an Egyptian passport, it will be difficult for me. Of course, the U.S. will not kick me out, but as my documents are not ready, I cannot bring my husband here. My asylum application has been rejected three times. The reason they give is, "you are fighting the Chinese government, but you have no problem with the Egyptian government." I tried to explain that the Egyptian government can extradite me to China. It is difficult if you don't have the green card or citizenship in the U.S. You need to renew your driving license every year, renew your work permit, and you can't apply for good jobs.

Mihrigul spoke about her uneasy place in the diasporic Uyghur community. Although she has been warmly embraced by human rights groups and other Uyghur activists, she noted that "many people are scared of me here in Virginia. They turn their faces away when they see me." She explained:

> There are other concentration camp witnesses who were able to escape China and arrive in the U.S. But they are not speaking out. Uyghur organizations helped them come to the U.S., but they don't want to speak out, they stay away from politics. Uyghurs in the diaspora are already in trouble, and they don't want to lose contact with their family back home.
>
> I will tell you one thing. If one person speaks out against the Chinese government, it will affect everyone for the next six generations in the family. The Chinese government enacted such a law in 2016. Six generations of the family cannot go to university, cannot work in the government, cannot get a passport, and a lot of other rules … For example, in my case, my parents, my siblings, their spouses, their children and grandchildren will all have a big problem.

We asked Mihrigul if she were in touch with other Uyghur women activists. She replied, "Yes, I meet with other Uyghur women activists often and work with them." When we asked her if she thought women could be equally effective as men in the political arena, she responded with passion:

> Definitely, maybe more than men sometimes. We do more than men, I think. Women are emotional, they don't think too much, they make decisions quickly when they want to do something. Men think too much before doing something. For example, when I left China, my brother cried and said, "think about me, my children, our parents [before you do anything]." I told him "I love you and my family, but I don't just think about you, I have to think about all the

Uyghur people. I have to become the voice of the Uyghur people." I have realized that if everyone keeps quiet, then the whole Uyghur people will be gone. I have to become the voice of those who are in the concentration camps, and those who have already died in them.

Three Turning Points

There were three turning points in Mihrigul's narrative. The first was when she disseminated the controversial video that sparked the 2009 Urumqi Incident. The second was when the police took away her baby triplets, drilled holes in their necks and killed the strongest boy while crippling the surviving two babies. Mihrigul insists, "They were not sick before. On the plane [to Beijing] they played with me, they could smile, they took my breast milk. When the Chinese took them, they couldn't have breast milk, they were only two months old at the time. [When I got them back] the condition they were in was very bad." The third turning point was when she witnessed the deaths of nine inmates in her cell while she was in prison:

> What I saw in the prison; I saw my teacher, my neighbor, my aunt, their daughters—girls as young as me, or younger than me—had all lost their children. It is not only me, a lot of people lost their children. My cell number was 210 in the prison. I counted there were more than two hundred cells in the prison where I was locked up. There were sixty people in my cell only. Within three months, nine women died in my cell. Think about how many people died in other cells? [Mihrigul estimated that 1,890 people died every three months in that prison, totaling 7,560 deaths a year.]
>
> In the prison, I prayed to Allah that if I get a second chance, get out alive, I promise that I will fight this evil power forever and be the voice of those people who died unjustly.[lix] Allah gave me a second life, and every time I do something those people who died will be happy with me. Actually, what I have done is not enough, I need to do more. Some people tell me that I need to stop, but no, I will never stop. I think this is what Allah destined me to do for the rest of my life. I have lost everything—my father and mother, my youth, my home, my education. But I am here now in this free country, I can speak—but my people, they cannot speak. Many people have died because they had no voice, and there are millions of people still suffering. If I keep silent, then they will die too. I need the whole world to know how horrible China is!

Mihrigul spoke about her work since arriving in the U.S. to raise public awareness about the genocide:

> I spoke at the United Nations and at the Uyghur Tribunal. We protested for three days in front of the White House. I have given more than 425 interviews to different news outlets, universities, and in many languages, Uyghur, Chinese, English, Arabic. I spent more than a year with a German writer to write my biography. It is going to be published in January next year.[ix] A Japanese woman is also writing my story. There are three books in Uyghur about my life. I am happy for that.

When we asked about her plans for the future, Mihrigul declared:

> My purpose is, I will fight the Chinese government for the rest of my life. I will raise my kids to know that they are Uyghur, that China killed their brother, and that they must fight the Chinese government after I die until we take back our Homeland. I will never hide. They tried to hit my car, and I have moved to six different places in the U.S. They tried to send letters to my home, to take pictures of me at the mall, they forced my parents and siblings to say that I am a liar. But everything I tell is true. I have the documents with me to prove it. I will make the whole world understand that the Chinese government is horrible and a liar.
>
> I will never stop, if a person in the street asks me, I will explain to him or her about my country and what happened to my people. I am studying now and will be working soon. I just work for my children, I just want a normal life. You might think that I am sick, many people think so. I am not sick, I need to let people know about this, even if it is to wake up one person. Sometimes I worry that I might not see any Uyghurs if I go back to my country. Some people don't understand or cannot imagine the situation. Maybe if you were in my place, you might do more than me. I am just one woman, and I can only do this. I have health problems, I was injected with many bad things in the prison. Doctors say if I stop taking medicine for one month, I might get blood cancer. I don't care, this is from Allah. I take my medicine and do what I can. I lost my hearing in my right ear, I only hear from my left ear. But thank God, I didn't lose my tongue. I can still speak. I will be fighting the Chinese government as long as I live until we take back our Homeland.

Part Three

Restorying a Genocide

In what sense are these formidable female Uyghurs "restorying" a genocide? To address this question, we must first explore the meaning of "restorying" and how it applies to the Uyghurs.

Restorying is the process of constructing new meanings from old, "official" narratives. The process involves gathering stories, analyzing their key elements, filling in missing information, and then rewriting the story. Genevieve Boast offers an eloquent account of this process, and she argues that restorying is a call to social action:

> Our human world is made of stories [flowing] through the veins of our societies like blood … They are our primary way of making sense of our experiences and the course of our lives, [both] personally and collectively. The telling of stories is an ancient art form. They can appear ingrained and hard to change but the reality is that our stories are themselves in a constant process of evolution … just like life. All we need to consciously change them are the keys and practices that move us from the ethereal world of … words into the tangible, material world of actions.[i]

Mary DeMocker presents the concept of "re-storying" as a method of organizing activist engagement. Restorying, she claims, is a resource used by the downtrodden to construct powerful new narratives that replace the "tried and true" stories that support injustice, corporate abuse of power, and government negligence.[ii] Techniques of "restorying" have been applied by psychiatrists in therapeutic settings and by sociologists in the research field.[iii] More importantly, "restorying" was part of the process of the Truth and Reconciliation Commission's effort to reconcile Canada's Indigenous peoples with the white settlers and their colonialist government. The TRC gathered testimonies from First Nations, Inuit and Métis from 300 communities over a span of six years; testimonies of at least

6,000 Indigenous women and men who were abused as children in the residential school system for the 2015 report, titled *Honouring the Truth, Reconciling for the Future.*[iv]

Uyghurs in the diaspora are currently engaged in the creative process of "restorying." It is through deconstructing the old [Chinese] narratives and constructing new ones, by voicing their individual truths and sharing a common truth that they are finding a way—perhaps the only way—to expose the egregious crimes against humanity ongoing in their Homeland in their attempt to rescue what is left of their people.

Our ten narrators contribute to this restorying process in several ways. They are providing their Western audience with close-up glimpses of the Uyghur experience in the decades that preceded the harsher genocidal policies of the Chinese government since the 2014 "Strike Hard" campaign; the 2017 "re-education" camps; and the 2019 forcible sterilizations. Their stories put a human face on the subtle political trends behind China's Great Firewall in the early twenty-first century. Their vivid anecdotes describe crowds of Han settlers arriving *en masse* on buses to invade villages and cities in their Homeland, how the Xinjiang government appropriated farms and orchards belonging to Uyghur families' ancestral land, and how individuals cope with high-tech surveillance and constant checkpoints; these anecdotes convey a sense of immediacy. They evoke the horror and injustice of China's oppressive regime and as such, they are more likely to awaken the conscience of the West.

What renders these women's stories credible is that each tale is told from the individual's unique perspective—and yet, as one reads through the ten testimonies, the same themes, the same moments in history reappear, albeit viewed from slightly different angles. It is as if each woman is offering us her own piece of a vast jigsaw puzzle that fits in neatly with its adjacent pieces.

Our ten narrators offer vivid glimpses of what it was like for Uyghurs in the 1990s, living in East Turkestan/Xinjiang, or studying in Shanghai or Guangzhou. The situations they describe remind us of other "unfree" peoples: African Americans under the "Jim Crow" laws, Blacks during the *apartheid* regime in South Africa, and the Palestinians in Zionist Israel.[v]

Eight of these narratives follow a similar trajectory; the women briefly recount their early life, then move on to describe their university experiences, their struggles to find meaningful employment after graduating, the events that precipitated their choices to emigrate to the West, and how they joined the Uyghur advocacy movement and carved out a meaningful life in the diaspora.

We have chosen to call these women "activists" for lack of a better term. It must be recognized that, during their interviews, Rushan Abbas, Dilnur Reyhan,

Gulchehra Hoja, and Rukiye Turdush all rejected this label, claiming it distorted or trivialized the meaning of their work. Gulchehra Hoja objected to being called an "activist" because she is a journalist and therefore required to maintain a stance that is unbiased and objective. In contrast, Rahima Mahmut, Zubayra Shamseden, Arzu Gul, and Raziya Mahmut were all proud to call themselves "activists." Zumrat Dawat and Mihrigul Tursun offered no objections to this label, but they more accurately fit the description of *whistleblower* ("an individual who, without authorization, reveals private or classified information about an organization, usually related to wrongdoing or misconduct").[vi] These two women are camp survivors who, unlike some of the other women, never studied International Relations or previously worked with human rights student groups, but each has exhibited a passionate commitment to "becoming the voice of my people" and has spoken out against the Chinese government at the United Nations, at press conferences, and at the Uyghur Tribunal.[vii] In this respect they qualify as "activists" who rely on the authority gained from their direct experience as camp survivors.

Six of these women studied at the top universities in Mainland China. Rushan Abbas and Gulchehra Hoja pursued their higher education at Xinjiang University respectively. Mihrigul Tursun attended university in Cairo. Zumrat Dawat married early, had children, managed a business, and never went to university. For Uyghurs to study in the top ten universities on the mainland was uncommon, especially in the 1990s, when most Uyghurs would have done their post-secondary education in East Turkestan/Xinjiang. To provide some historical context here, the scholarships awarded to students living in East Turkestan/Xinjiang were part of an academic initiative later known at the High School level as "Xinjiang Class." Xinjiang Class was ostensibly created to offer ethnic-minority students' higher education and job training. However, as Timothy Grose points out in his 2019 book *Negotiating Inseparability in China*, "political goals [were] often emphasized over the mastery of any subject." He argues that the PRC's real purpose was to "train a cohort of ethnic minority intellectuals who are sympathetic to the Chinese Communist Party (CCP) and its state-building projects in Xinjiang."[viii]

Timothy Grose describes how the Uyghur graduate students he interviewed "complained bitterly about the few job prospects available to them in their homeland, many of which—they insisted—would be subordinate to Han employers and managers." Grose also notes that, "these programs resemble boarding schools established in North America and Australia, which attempted [...] to assimilate indigenous peoples."[ix]

Thus, despite their Chinese education, ostensibly intended to offer them greater opportunity, these women were held back by their Uyghur ethnic identity, just like Grose's informants. The frustrations during their fruitless job searches resulted in a sense of disillusionment and a greater awareness of how Uyghurs were marginalized and subordinated by the state because they were identifiably Uyghur. Their sense of injustice is eloquently expressed in their interviews.

Uyghurs have been arriving in the West since the late 1980s. Some were skilled immigrants, others were asylum seekers, some arrived on tourist visas, and many on international student visas. They arrived in the West with meager economic resources, wielding minimal political influence. How could they fight back against their Chinese oppressors? The only weapon they possessed was their powerful, compelling stories.

Restorying involves innovation, in terms of finding an audience and new media to convey the stories.[x] Gulchehra Hoja hosts radio programs and writes stories for Radia Free Asia. Rushan Abbas and her missing sister are the subjects of a documentary film. Zubayra Shamseden networks with pro-democracy Chinese-speaking groups. Sympathetic allies in the West, filmmakers, biographers, journalists, and comic artists are facilitating these women's storytelling process.

Tomomi Shimizu, a Japanese artist, has employed her manga cartoon skills to relate the harrowing story of Mihrigul Tursun, one of the first camp survivors to escape to the West. Shimizu's manga went "viral," drawing public attention to the Chinese Communist Party's treatment of the Uyghurs.[xi] As Shimizu explained to Reuters, "The Uighur issue has been well known among people who are into politics. But little is known among the general public. The gap is staggering."[xii]

In an effort to lessen this "staggering gap," Uyghur advocacy groups in the West have been making a concerted effort to raise awareness of the mass detentions, forced sterilizations, torture, indoctrination, and relentless decimation of their people that is ongoing in East Turkestan/Xinjiang. And how do they do this? Through telling stories.

The Saga of a "Slow Genocide": Conflicting Sources of Information

China's draconian control over the Uyghurs has been in featured in the media since 2009, when the forcible demolition of the ancient city of Kashgar was reported in the *New York Times*.[xiii] Since then, the Western public has becoming increasingly aware of the "Uyghur crisis" through articles in prestigious and reliable media outlets.[xiv] What are the sources of information about what is going on inside China?

Chinese media outlets are tightly controlled by the Chinese Communist Party. The Great Firewall (防火长城), created by the People's Republic of China, combines legal actions with technology to regulate the internet domestically. Thus, Google, Facebook, and Western news outlets cannot be accessed by Chinese citizens. Moreover, the movements of foreign visitors inside China, whether they be journalists, students, diplomats, or tourists, are carefully monitored.

There are three distinct versions of the "Uyghur story." One version is told by Western scholars, another is told by agents of the Chinese government, and still another is told by Uyghur expatriates living in the diaspora.

China watchers in the West basically rely on three sources of information: aerial photography, "leaked" documents, and the testimonies of former camp detainees.

Aerial Photography. Aerial photographs taken in 2017 provide important empirical evidence of Xinjiang's internment camps.[xv] In May 2017, the site of a suspected internment camp in Shufu County was captured in satellite imagery by Shawn Zhang, a Chinese second-year law student at the University of British Columbia.[xvi] He found photographs of the newly built "re-education centers" on Baudu (Chinese version of Google) and plugged the coordinates into Google Earth for satellite images that showed the size and layout of the compounds.[xvii]

In September 2020, Nathan Ruser, a researcher at the Australian Strategic Policy Institute, after two years of scouring the satellite imagery, announced that the ASPI team had found 380 separate detention facilities "sprung out of the deserts and oases, or expanded from smaller detention facilities since 2017 ... The largest is more than 300 acres in size."[xviii]

Adrian Zenz has described these camps as: "prison-like compounds: surrounding walls, security fences, pull wire mesh, barbwire, reinforced security doors and windows, surveillance systems, secure access systems, watchtowers, guard rooms, police stations or facilities for armed police forces."[xix] Darren Byler notes, "by most estimates, about 10% of Uighurs and other Muslim nationalities in Xinjiang have found themselves arbitrarily detained in these camps."[xx]

Leaked Documents. The second source of information available to the West has been the "leaked" documents from government police files, or Chinese social media.

In November 2019 *The New York Times* ran a story on "leaked documents" smuggled out by refugees or provided by anonymous sources inside China; documents that revealed the Chinese government's deliberate strategy to reduce and assimilate the Uyghur population.[xxi] A major leak was the "Karakax list," which first arrived in the hands of Asiye Abdulaheb, a Uyghur intellectual living in Norway, who relayed it to Dr. Adrian Zenz and various Western media outlets. The Karakax list is a 137-page PDF generated from an Excel spreadsheet or Word table which contains data on hundreds of imprisoned Uyghurs from the Karakax region.[xxii]

A third important source was the cache of over 25,000 local government files that Adrian Zenz somehow obtained and used to write his 2019 article, "Sterilizations, IUDs, and Mandatory Birth Control: The CCP's Campaign to Suppress Uyghur Birthrates in Xinjiang." These files include household registration documents from the Xinjiang government's family planning campaigns, as well as policy statements on population control, such as "Zero birth control violation incidents."[xxiii]

Timothy Grose of the Rose-Hulman Institute of Technology explored Chinese-language social media sites with connections to the Chinese Communist Party (CCP) to find data on the mass incarcerations and the impact on the Xinjiang region's Turkic communities:

> County-level social media accounts and cadre blogs describe how the party-state detained Uyghurs and Kazakhs without due process, held them in inhumane conditions, separated scores of children from their parents, and imposed policies to destroy ethno-religious identities.[xxiv]

Grose concludes, "Chinese social media sources maintained by the CCP … and made publicly available at the Xinjiang Documentation Project (2022)—incriminate the party-state in an open-and-shut case of serious human rights violations committed against Uyghurs and Kazakhs."[xxv]

The most recent and valuable cache of leaked documents are the "Xinjiang Police Files," a major cache of classified files obtained by a third party from internal XUAR police networks. Adrian Zenz was behind the discovery of the Xinjiang Police Files, published on May 24, 2022 by several international media.[xxvi] Zenz announced triumphantly, "It's the first time we have police evidence that is unfiltered. It comes from hacking, so censorship is virtually impossible." He obtained several thousand computer files containing the records of 20,000 Uighurs who were arrested. The files contain 5,000 photos of Uyghurs aged between 3 and 94 years old, along with countless instructions, briefings, and police reports dating from between 2000 and 2018 in Xinjiang. The data trove was extracted from hacked servers of the public security bureau (PSB) in two districts of the region.[xxvii] The cache of documents includes speeches by Chen Quanguo, the Chinese Communist Party's secretary for Xinjiang, as well as detailed security instructions for special police units carrying military assault weapons with photographs of guards handcuffing detainees. Recorded speeches by leading officials advise the camp guards to treat the detainees like dangerous criminals; to readily open fire on prisoners trying to escape.[xxviii] Adrian Zenz concludes, "These files show just how paranoid Chinese authorities are about alleged terrorist dangers from Uighurs—from the bottom to the top of the hierarchical ladder."[xxix]

Camp Survivors' Testimonies

The third source of information is found in the testimonies of former detainees who were released from the camps and subsequently escaped from China. These are frequently cited in media, in government reports, and by Uyghur human rights groups. A testament to the camp survivors' power of storytelling was given by the Georgia Embassy in Tbilisi on February 22, 2022:

> Recent events indicate that PRC internment survivors' stories are having an effect. In October 2021, the United States, France, Luxembourg, Belgium and 39 other countries, in a joint statement at the United Nations, urged the PRC to respect human rights and allow independent observers "immediate, meaningful and unfettered access" to Xinjiang, citing reports of arbitrary detention and other abuses.[xxx]

James Millward sums up the camp survivors' testimonies as follows: "They report crowded cells, unsanitary conditions, poor food, beatings, physical and psychological torture, and systematic rape, as well as forced sterilization, IUD-implantation, and administration of anti-fertility drugs."[xxxi] Darren Byler notes that survivors' testimonies clearly indicate that their detentions were arbitrary and extralegal, without indictments or a fair trial.[xxxii]

The first camp survivor who described life inside Xinjiang's "re-education" camps was Omir Bekali, a Uyghur whose testimony appeared in May 2018 in *The Associated Press*.[xxxiii] Since late 2018, the harrowing experiences of other Uyghur or Kazakhs who have been detained can be read in *The New York Times*, *The Guardian*, *The Washington Post*, the BBC,[xxxiv] or in the hearings at the United Nations.[xxxv]

The "Uyghur Story" as Told by Academics in the West

The broadest, most coherent narrative of the "slow genocide" is being constructed by Western academics and research groups. While China maintains an opaque front towards its own citizens and the outside world, scholars in various West countries, anthropologists, sinologists, Tibetologists, Islamicists, or historians of Uyghur culture, have significantly shaped the reports on Xinjiang issued by major news outlets.[xxxvi]

In 2014 James A. Millward wrote an op-ed for *The New York Times* which described an "intense crackdown" on Uyghurs by Xinjiang authorities following a sporadic series of student demonstrations and violent protests by Uyghur nationalists.[xxxvii] This "crackdown" included "house-to-house searches, and a campaign against traditional symbols of [Muslim] identity: veils, beards, traditional hats, fasting, prayer." Millward concludes: "combined with the recent razing of Uighur architecture in the ancient city of Kashgar and elimination of the Uighur-language educational track from Xinjiang's schools and universities, these measures seem aimed at repressing Uighur culture."[xxxviii]

Connor W. Dooley from the University of Georgia School of Law identifies the 2014 "intense crackdown" as a "Strike Hard" campaign. "Strike Hard" was a police tactic, first implemented as a method to deter crime across China in Spring 1996.[xxxix] Under Chen Quanguo, Xinjiang's new Party Secretary, Strike Hard involved raids targeting Uyghur neighborhoods in which Uyghur literature, music, religious texts, and any material in the Uyghur language would be seized and burned. Those in possession of materials considered by the government as propagating "extremism" would be arrested.[xl] Dooley notes:

> Strike Hard is historically a discriminatory tactic devoted largely to the suppression of cultural dissidents. It is clearly illegal under both the international agreements and the integral rights implicated in Xinjiang. The core premise and motivating force behind Strike Hard is the elimination of dissidents, and the Uyghurs, who have been motivated by religious ideas and the distant memory of self-rule, are its natural targets.[xli]

The PRC's motives for this repression have been explored by journalists and scholars. The Organization for World Peace has proposed three reasons why China regards the Uyghur people as "extremely problematic." First, they happen to reside in the signature region for the Belt and Road Initiative.[xlii] Second, they have a high procreation rate. Third, Uyghurs are a Muslim minority.[xliii]

James Millward observed, "The ultimate goal, the ultimate issue, is that the Chinese state is targeting the cultural practices and beliefs of Muslim groups." He argues the main purpose is "to expunge ethnonational characteristics from the people. They're not trying to drive them out of the country; they're trying to hold them in."

Adrian Zenz and Darren Byler have each proposed that the recent history of Uyghurs in China is an epic story of a mass assimilation program, facilitated by an unprecedented level of technological surveillance. Zenz dubs it "a mass social re-engineering project that's trying to change a people."[xliv] For Byler, "the term I might use [instead of 'cultural genocide'] is *social engineering* ... it goes beyond just the cultural erasure ... *all* of the basic institutions of Uyghur society are being transformed ... their religion and the family, and also language."[xlv] Millward offers a detailed account of this "mass social engineering experiment" as follows:

> Uyghur, Kazakh, Kyrgyz, and Uzbek internees have not been tried before internment, but simply accused of extremism. Signs of supposed extremism, published in a list used by police for the purpose of identifying "precrimes" in potential internees, include such mundane Islamic practices as avoiding alcohol, fasting, veiling, wearing a beard, or owning a Quran. Foreign travel or contacts and having "too many children" are also justifications for detention. Within the camps, internees are subjected to regimented daily routines, political indoctrination, some Mandarin language training, and forced renunciations of Islam and Uyghur culture.[xlvi]

In a recent (February 2023) interview, Millward comments on a new development; many of the infamous re-education camps are being shut down. He suggests that the PRC seems to be "transitioning away from camps and extra-legal detention, but that its detention and control of people is not over, that many are transferred to prisons, forced labour camps, and Uyghur exiles report that their relatives have been sent home to live under house arrest." He interprets this trend as an "admission that the camps were very obvious to the West and drew a lot of attention," and that "no one anticipated they would be compared to concentration camps."[xlvii]

Several scholars have tried to plummet the Chinese government's "mindset" towards the Uyghurs. Sean Roberts (2020) suggests that Beijing perceives the Uyghurs as a type of "biological threat" to society; a threat that must be contained.[xlviii] David Tobin notes how the Chinese state exacerbates the tensions between ethnic groups through exaggerated threat portrayals and securitizing strategies: "Persons like Chen can come to view re-education camps as institutions that reflect the kindness of the state and where living conditions are comparatively decent, filtering out any information to the contrary that they may have received from their subordinates."[xlix]

Adrian Zenz has added a new dimension to the academic scrutiny of Xinjiang's "slow genocide" by delving into the psychological motivations of Chinese government officials. Relying on theories in the field of social psychology, Zenz proposes that the pre-emptive mass internment of ordinary Xinjiang citizens "who just happen to belong to ethnic minorities" can be explained as "a devolution into political paranoia that promotes exaggerated threat perceptions."[1]

Zenz points out that China's rapid development of securitization and surveillance systems, initially designed to control terrorists or violent criminals, are now being used to micromanage and punish "wide swaths of the population." While previous scholarly interpretations of what Zenz calls the "slow genocide" in Xinjiang have "tended to frame state discourses of counterterrorism as a propagandistic façade concealing ulterior political or financial motives,"[li] he argues that events in Xinjiang need to be examined in light of the state's changing perception of the international and domestic terrorism threat.[lii]

Since there is a scholarly consensus that the terrorist incidents were rare—hardly in proportion to the "de-extremification" measures that followed—Zenz claims the scale of Xinjiang's re-education campaign reflect a "devolution into paranoia." He cites Dirk Moses, who analyzed pre-emptive strikes against a perceived threat group as an "interpretative disorder constituted by hysterical threat assessments."[liii] Zenz suggests that President Xi, Chen Quanguo, XUAR administrators, and police chiefs have all "thoroughly internalized" the official state discourses on terrorism and extremism. He cites Robins and Post, who argue that the paranoid–schizoid position uses projective identification and splitting to project the hated parts of the self out and onto the "Other," while simultaneously idealizing the good within oneself.[liv] Zenz then concludes:

> This psychological defense mechanism can explain how Xi Jinping, Chen Quanguo, and other leaders came to frame Uyghurs as a pathological threat, while simultaneously portraying themselves as their kind benefactors. The paranoid focus on the potential for threat residing in non-violent but not yet "de-extremified" Uyghur citizens, might explain Chen's literal obsession with the "absolute security" of already highly securitized internment facilities. No camp survivor has ever testified about successful escapes, but rather about abuse, starvation, complete hopelessness, and the suffering, especially of the elderly. This vast cognitive dissonance between the state's extreme security measures *vis-à-vis* the helpless state of the detainees is precisely a product of the delusional threat assessment generated by the paranoid mind.[lv]

The Uyghur Story, as Told by the Chinese Government

The official Chinese narrative, expressed in *The Global Times* (a daily tabloid newspaper under the auspices of the Chinese Communist Party's flagship) typically follows this argument:

> The Uyghurs of Xinjiang are a backward people, still clinging to religious beliefs that alienate them from the True Ideology of the PRC. Their communities are hotbeds of terrorism and extremism. In order to alleviate their poverty and ignorance, the PRC has built "re-education facilities" where Uyghurs receive "vocational education and training" and study the basic elements of Marxism, Maoism and Xi Jinping.

The Chinese official narrative, however, has been periodically revised. Initially, government officials flatly denied the existence of internment camps, but after images of camp construction with watch towers and barbed wire fences were clearly visible via aerial photography, the government acknowledged the presence of "re-education" or "vocational training centers" for Uyghurs that were "voluntary."[lvi] Today, they are claiming the camps are being shut down because all the "happy Uyghurs" have "graduated" and have found meaningful work in industry (actually forced labor and slave-like conditions in Xinjiang's cotton fields and factory compounds).

Chinese ambassadors in the West issue press statements that roundly dismiss criticism of PRC policies and all allegations of human rights violations. Cong Peiwu, Ambassador to Canada, in March 2021, dismissed rumors of genocide against the Uyghurs, and called the allegations of forced labor and detention camps "the lies of the century."[lvii]

Different methods are used to challenge the credibility of China's critics. *The Global Times* does this by applying a liberal sprinkling of quotation marks, as in the August 5, 2021 statement (*"Things to Know about All the Lies on Xinjiang"*) by the Consulate-General of the PRC in Toronto:

> In recent years, manipulated and encouraged by the anti-China forces in the United States, some truth-bending "academic institutions," rumour-mongering "experts and scholars" and "amateur actors" with no moral scruples have created a chain of lies to defame Xinjiang and misled international public discourse, often through dirty funding, fact-twisting stories, and massive smear campaigns. Truth shall not be tainted.[lviii]

A second way to handle criticisms is to claim they are based on ignorance, as in the statement by a Chinese Embassy spokesperson after Canada's Parliament passed a resolution that China's treatment of the Uyghurs qualified as a "genocide":

> Some Canadian politicians have never been to ... China before, but they have engaged in political manipulation on Xinjiang-related issues, under the pretext of human rights, disseminating false information and lies.

A third strategy is *rationalization*; the attempt to *justify* the behavior being criticized. The same Chinese Embassy spokesperson deflects criticism by rationalizing China's excessive control measures: "Xinjiang has not seen a terrorist incident for over four years because it is ruled in such a way as to counter violence and terrorism and for deradicalization."[lix]

Chinese foreign ministry spokesman, Geng Shuang, responding to Mike Pompeo's 2018 statement at the UN, declared:

> Xinjiang is an internal affair, and the issue there is not a religious or ethnic one, but about preventing terror and separatism. China has not relied on starting wars to deal with terrorism, but has used education and training, in accordance with the law, to help people who have been influenced by extremist and terrorist thinking return to society and a normal life. We hope that certain U.S. politicians can remove their colored spectacles, cast aside double standards and stop using Xinjiang-related issues to attack and defame China's words and actions.[lx]

In a similar rationalizing effort, after Adrian Zenz' explosive 2019 article on the forcible mass sterilization of Uyghur women came out, the Chinese Embassy in Washington, D.C. tweeted: "Uyghur women in Xinjiang are now emancipated, they are no longer baby making machines."[lxi] Thus, the forcible mass sterilizations of Uyghur women was recast as a wise birth control policy that emancipated Uyghur women so that they could join the work force and lead more fulfilling lives.[lxii]

A fourth method used is the *ad hominem* attack, of which Adrian Zenz is a frequent butt. Under the headline, "Xinjiang think tank unveils Adrian Zenz as swindler under academic disguise," *The Global Times* challenged Zenz's scholarly credentials by name calling and a sprinkling of quotation marks:

> Zenz, is a Christian evangelical eschatologist who believes that he is "led by God" on a "mission" against China ... Cobbling together dubious sources ... his "reports" [on] "detaining" Uyghurs or imposing "sterilization" on ethnic minorities, Zenz has been welcomed by ... Western media as a "leading expert" on Xinjiang. Zenz' "reports" ... cited and hyped by ... Western media are full

of lies, farfetched assumptions, and baseless accusations. These reports ... have proven to be false, time and time again.[lxiii]

Elijan Anayat, a spokesperson of the People's Government of XUAR, also launched an *ad hominem* attack on Zenz, as a reaction to his article on the Xinjiang Police Files:[lxiv]

> First, Adrian Zenz has long been notorious in the world. He is a member of ... a far right-wing organization funded by the U.S. government and once known as the shelter of new Nazis, fascists and anti-Semitic extremists ... [He] has a sense of mission to oppose China and is "led by God to do this". With such an evil intention, he published a number of Xinjiang-related reports ... based on speculation, imagination and conjecture ... Adrian Zenz is doing his old tricks again to play up the so-called Xinjiang Police Files, which just further exposes his conspiracy of destabilizing Xinjiang.[lxv]

A fifth defensive strategy used by the Chinese government is to seek out its critics' relatives who are living in China and forcibly persuade them to denounce their activist kin in the West. This might be dubbed the *forced witness* strategy. Mihrigul Tursun's brother, interviewed by the *China Global Television Network*, branded her as a liar ("My sister never went to the education and training center. She made that up, it is a lie").[lxvi] Zumrat Dawut's brother, Abduhelil, stated in a video interview with *The Global Times*, "these are outright lies ... my sister has never been to a vocational education and training center, and when delivering the third child, she was found to have fibroids and later had a surgery."[lxvii] In a similar fashion, Gulchehra Hoja's mother and brother were also forced to denounce her.

The Uyghur Story as Told by Uyghur Expatriates

The third version of the Uyghur story is being told by Uyghur expatriates; individuals who have left China and are living abroad as refugees or landed immigrants residing in Europe, North America, or Australia. The considerable majority are neither camp survivors nor overt "activists." They are "ordinary Uyghurs," intent on adjusting to life in democratic Western societies, while deeply concerned about the fate of East Turkestan, their Homeland. Because they care about the well-being of relatives in China, they keep a low profile. However, many of these "ordinary Uyghurs" are secretly contributing to the Uyghur advocacy movement by using digital methods, low-tech and open-source, to retrieve, archive, and circulate information about what they call the "concentration camps." These methods favor immediacy, transparency, and collaboration.

A good example is an ordinary Uyghur woman [pseudonym: "Nur"] who is described in Samuel Sigal's article in *The Atlantic*. She was the very first researcher to dig up what is now a widely circulated image showing inmates in an internment camp in Lop County, Hotan, Xinjiang. Nur found this and other photos by sifting through accounts published by the government's official account on WeChat, a Chinese social media platform.[lxviii]

Timothy Grose explains how these amateurish methods reflect the urgency of the situation.[lxix]

> The platforms that we have for academic writing take so long. To get an article published, you have to count on at least a year. We don't have the luxury to wait a year with what's going on in Xinjiang right now … This is a race against time, so we have to use the tools that are going to give us the most immediate and effective results.[lxx]

The Uyghur Story, as Told by Uyghur Women Activists

Our ten women activists have been constantly challenging China's official "story" regarding its treatment of Uyghurs, some of them since childhood.

Zubayra, Rukiye, and Arzu, as university students, boldly challenged the Communist Party's revisionist view of history; the notion that "Xinjiang has always been part of China." Arzu had naively assumed that, because she was in an academic setting, the evidence she found to support her claims would be sufficient to dispel any false notions. However, both she and Rukiye quickly realized that the state's official history was the only "truth" that mattered.

Rushan Abbas provides her own restorying of East Turkestan's history in her 2021 interview:

> The Uyghurs have lived in Central Asia for thousands of years … The ancient Silk Road in the Uyghur kingdom [was] a prominent center of commerce for more than 2000 years. But the Manchus invaded … East Turkestan, in 1876 and renamed the area "Xinjiang." In Chinese, that means "new territory" or "new border." The Uyghurs staged numerous uprisings against Chinese rule and twice established the East Turkestan Republic, once in 1933 and again in 1944. We called it "East Turkestan" because Uyghurs are Turkic people. But the CCP occupied our homeland in 1949. Now, it is officially part of China. Uyghurs

were persecuted in the 1950s as "nationalists" ... in the 1960s as "counter revolutionaries" ... in the 1980s and 90s as "separatists." After 9/11 China ... used the war on terror as a pretext to persecute us as Muslims. Today's genocide is because of Xi Jinping's signature projects for world domination. China's Belt and Road Initiative puts our homeland in the epicenter of this important project ... the gateway to Central Asia, Europe, Africa, and the Middle East. Instead of working with local people, the [PRC] decided this is an opportunity to get rid of the Uyghurs for good. China uses its ... Belt and Road Initiative to keep the nations they have invested in silent.[lxxi]

Rushan Abbas poses frequent challenges to the Chinese state's claim that the Uyghurs of Xinjiang are "happy and free." In her interview with the George W. Bush Presidential center, she describes contemporary China as a high-tech distopia:

Even people living so-called normal lives outside of the camps are subject to the ultra-nationalistic racism and cutting-edge technology that the authorities are using to control the Uyghur people. Everybody's subject to cameras on every corner and facial recognition software that scans your iris. There are GPS tracking devices on every vehicle, as well as QR scanning codes on everybody's home. That's the reality for the Uyghur people today, inside and outside of the camps.[lxxii]

Rushan Abbas also denounces the Chinese government's debilitating attack on Uyghur motherhood and the integrity of Uyghur family life:

More than 900,000 Uyghur children have been abducted from their families and taken into state-run orphanages. And Uyghur women are forced to marry Han Chinese people. If they refuse a forced marriage to Han Chinese men, whom the government gives a job, housing, and money to marry Uyghur women and girls, the women will be taken to those concentration camps. They will be labeled as Islamic extremists who didn't want to marry non-Muslim Han Chinese.[lxxiii]

Gulchehra, as a rejoinder to the Chinese government's boast that their policies have "liberated" and "modernized" Uyghur women from being treated as "baby-making machines," spoke about women as prime the targets in the Uyghur genocide:

Women have been the symbols of our culture, of our Uyghur identity. They were considered as guards of the mother language, belief, and culture. But the Chinese government wants control of the Uyghur woman's body, soul, and to take her children. It was not enough that China's strict birth control policy put severe pressure on our women, punishing them for having an extra child. Next, there was forced sterilization. In 2017 the government sent out one million cadres [Chinese officials] to live in Uyghur homes, to live with families and force them to eat pork with them. This is called the "Five Together" policy, designed to control their lives. "Five Together" policy is five things: "eat, cook, live, study, work, and sleep together"—the most ridiculous thing I ever heard!

Women have been relocated to far off provinces under the guise of employment opportunities, and now they are put in forced labour camps. Many are forced to get married to Chinese men, or even trafficked in prostitution rings. Since 2017, a million women have been in concentrations camp where forced organ harvesting of the prisoners is an industry. But physical trauma is nothing compared to the psychological trauma inflicted on mothers who have no idea where their children are, or even if they are alive or not. We are rapidly losing a whole generation in this nightmare environment.[lxxiv]

The Uyghur Tribunal

Restorying is a dialectical process. One can observe a struggle to own the truth by watching how the Chinese government reacts to the statements of Uyghur activists and academics, and how the latter respond to these denials. This dialectical process reached its peak with the Uyghur Tribunal.

The Uyghur Tribunal was an independent people's tribunal that was launched in London on September 2020 by Sir Geoffrey Nice, the former prosecutor in the war crimes trial of Slobodan Milošević. As Sir Geoffrey Nice explained, the verdict of this tribunal was not legally binding, but it was a response to a global concern about China's treatment of the Muslim minorities in China. Dolkun Isa, president of the World Uyghur Congress, had requested this civic forum because international courts and the Chinese legal system have no mechanisms by which the claims of Uyghurs (or indeed of any minority peoples) could be heard without consent of the accused party—in this case, the PRC. No government was willing to share evidence, and the tribunal's specific requests to the U.S.A., United Kingdom, and Japan had already been declined.[lxxv]

The Uyghur Tribunal's stated purpose was to investigate crimes against humanity and genocide under international law, allegedly perpetrated by the Chinese state against Uyghurs, Kazakhs, and other Turkic-speaking Muslims in north-western China.

More than a dozen experts and a handful of witnesses joined the tribunal to present evidence, including former detainees of internment camps in Xinjiang, and Western scholars.

The Global Times condemned the Uyghur Tribunal as a "maverick pseudo-court," and accused the three British MPs (sanctioned by China) who attended the press conference to publicize its "ruling" of "venting anger at China." "The British parliament should feel shameful [*sic*] about those MPs," the article concludes, "the anti-China movement initiated by the US is becoming hysterical. The boundary of reason has been washed away, and Pandora's Box has been opened."[lxxvi]

Xu Guixiang, a spokesperson of the Xinjiang regional government, was quoted in *The Global Times* saying, "The so-called tribunal … gets money mainly from the WUC and presets guilty conclusions, using the lies of a bunch of anti-China 'scholars' and 'actresses and actors' to fool the public."[lxxvii]

On December 9, 2021, the tribunal issued its judgment: that "hundreds of thousands of Uyghurs—perhaps over a million—have been detained by PRC authorities without any, or any remotely sufficient reason, and subjected to acts of unconscionable cruelty, depravity and inhumanity."

The Turning Points

Each narrative contains one or more *turning points* that prompted our narrators' exit from China. If we compare the triggering moments that led to their escape scenarios, these women's experiences are strikingly similar. Eight women experienced a build up of tension (psychological and social) during their careers as university students and job-seeking graduates. Several were assigned to low-ranking jobs, despite their impressive credentials.

The aspect of "public" humiliation in their turning points is an important element because, besides attacking Uyghur identity, it serves to support the existing narrative in place in the Han Chinese community, that Uyghurs are to be perceived in a derogatory manner and thus are to be shamed for being Uyghur. Raziya describes how she was "outed" as a potential pickpocket while shopping in the mall. Rahima shares her humiliating experience of being turned away by five hotels during a train connection on her way to a conference. Arzu recounts how she was forced to dance in public with a dance troupe, hold hands with men and smile, to pose as a "happy Uyghur."

Lieblich, Tuval-Maschiach, and Zilber describe *turning points* as "life events experienced as critical moments or crucial periods of transitions."[lxxviii] Clausen notes they often present opportunities for reorienting or reinterpreting one's life.[lxxix] Bruner observes that autobiographies typically have turning points so that the protagonist-hero completes his/her story "aroused by victory or defeat, by betrayal or trust."[lxxx]

Turning points can be changes or movements in the storytelling which describe sequences or scenes as transitioning from better or worse. McAdams and Bowman see life's turning points as transitions that can move the storyline along a "redemption" sequence which they define as an "emotionally negative or bad scene to an emotionally positive or good outcome."[lxxxi] In contrast, a turning point can also move the narrative in reverse, that is from good to bad; this movement is categorized as a "contamination" sequence.[lxxxii] McAdams and Bowman explain that a contamination sequence is "an emotionally positive or good experience [that] is spoiled, ruined, sullied, or contaminated by a an emotionally negative or bad outcome."[lxxxiii]

A similar model is also echoed in Kenneth and Mary Gergen's typology of storytelling. The authors propose that storyline structures can be analyzed in terms of three basic narrative forms. The first is described as a *stability* narrative: this is "a narrative that links events in such a way that the individual remains essentially unchanged," thus the various events that lead to the end of a story do not move towards a positive or negative end goal.[lxxxiv] The second and third narrative forms are described as *progressive* and *regressive* respectively. In a *progressive* narrative sequence, "as one approaches the valued goal over time, the storyline becomes more positive," whereas in a *regressive* narrative sequence, "as one approaches failure, disillusionment, and so on, one moves in the negative direction."[lxxxv]

Our narrators' turning points fit the *regression* narrative sequence; of how life for Uyghurs in China was becoming worse and worse. Arzu tells the story of how her family's farmland was appropriated by the government and awarded to Han Chinese settlers. Rukiye describes losing her rebellious brother, who was killed by an XPCC mob. Mihrigul identifies two turning points in her narrative: first, when her oldest triplet, Muhannad, was taken by Chinese police and mysteriously died in hospital; and second, when she witnessed the death of nine women in her cell while she was held in prison. Gulchehra, Rahima, Rukiye, and Raziya each recount witnessing the traumatic aftermath of the Ghulja Incident.

For many of our narrators, the loss of contact with, or threats to their loved ones in China was a major turning point. They describe how their criticisms of the Chinese government set off reprisals against their loved ones and even distant relatives in China. Rushan's sister was "disappeared" after Rushan spoke up at a conference in Florida. Gulchehra's parents and aunts were arrested after she wrote an article for *Radio Free Asia* about a camp survivor. Rushan Abbas' father was punished after she spoke at a human rights conference.

None of these targeted relatives were found guilty of crimes; their only offense was they had kin living in the West who were deemed as "terrorists" or "enemies of China." These reprisals resemble "hostage diplomacy" and are quite inexplicable to a Western audience—unless one is aware of the Chinese concept of "family punishment."

As Rukiye Turdush explains in her 2021 article: "These kinds of punishments are referred to as the *lianzuo* or *zuxing* system, meaning shared responsibility and family penalty."[lxxxvi] The mutual responsibility policy started in 2013 in Kashgar, according to Turdush, and it is currently being widely applied to the people of East Turkestan. Daniel Haitas traces the concept of "family punishment" back to the fourth century BCE, where it is mentioned in *The Book of Lord Shang*, by Shang Yang, who was an official and a member of the Legalist school in the state of Qin.[lxxxvii] Raziya Mahmut refers to the concept of "family punishment" in her anecdote about a fellow passenger on her airplane who told her that Beijing had decreed: "If one Uyghur is disloyal to the Chinese Communist Party, then he and all his descendants will be punished until the third generation."

Narrative Time and Space

Given the current situation in East Turkestan/Xinjiang, these narratives could not have been constructed in the manner presented in this book if the women were still residing there. The fact that our interviews were conducted while they were living in Europe or North America made it possible to create a safe space for our research subjects to construct narratives in which they freely voiced their criticisms of the Chinese government. Kim Collins explains that narratives that are not part of what is understood as normative, or what we know to be socially acceptable, will be difficult, not only to tell, but to listen to.[lxxxviii]

In China, these women's narratives—which assert that every person has the same fundamental rights to freedom and equality, regardless of their ethnicity or religion—would be non-normative and therefore hard to tell (and to be heard). By providing the storyteller with a "safe space" to tell their narratives, the narrative then becomes an act, a tool which empowers the teller and leads to an effective form of activism.[lxxxix]

Imagined/Intended Audience

The oral narrative recounted by each of these women is a purposeful construction, directed towards an intended audience and told with a certain purpose in mind. As Frisk and Palmer note, a person's narrative cannot be regarded as simply fiction nor simply fact, for it involves a process of selection from assorted memories and creative interpretations of remembered events.[xc] Narratives are constructed in social settings and often draw upon cultural building blocks or traditional stories.

According to Bruner,[xci] our participants' autobiographical stories should not be understood as a means of telling us about who these women are, as there is no "essential self" waiting to be discovered; rather, autobiographical stories "constantly construct and reconstruct [the self] to meet the needs of the situation [encountered], and [are done] with the guidance of our memories of the past and our hopes and fears for the future."[xcii] Given our participants' hopes and fears for the future, we felt that even as they reflected on their youth in China, by emphasizing the discriminatory elements that they and their larger community faced in East Turkestan/Xinjiang, they were simultaneously "doing their jobs" as political activists. Their stories tell of the "everyday" systemic racism and discrimination that existed long before the contours of a genocide became visible, and it seems clear that their narratives—although perhaps not consciously or directly intended—can be meaningfully understood as a continuation of their advocacy and activism on behalf of their community.

This argument is further supported by William Gamson who explains that personal narratives "promote empathy across different social locations" by "reveal[ing] experiences based on social locations that cannot be shared fully by those who are differently situated."[xciii] In other words, as personal narratives "promote deliberation and dialogue in a narrative mode [… which] lends itself more easily to the expression of moral complexity,"[xciv] we argue that these women's narratives should be viewed as both a contribution to public discourse on the CCP's oppression of the Uyghurs, as well as an invitation for dialogue and policy development. The latter is of particular importance for, as Gamson notes, "narrative and experiential knowledge in a discourse does not translate into agency unless collective actors exist to tie the lessons of such stories to public policy."[xcv]

Narrative Means to Transformative Ends

Gamson argues that successfully mobilizing personal narratives towards political and social transformation is contingent upon collective actors demanding that public policy makers include these types of personal narratives in their deliberations. Survivors of the "re-education" camps—such as Mihrigul Tursun and Zumrat Dawut—have already accomplished this by sharing their stories while testifying in front of various political bodies, media outlets, and human rights organizations.[xcvi] We argue that our participants' stories contribute towards expanding the picture provided by these camp survivors. They deepen public awareness of how long-standing the CCP's marginalization and oppression of the Uyghurs has been.

The narratives recounted by each of these women are personal and they are stories about their lives they do not normally share. In fact, they told us that most of the stories they shared with us were recounted for the first time, since they were not accustomed to speaking about the details of their own lived experiences—each of the women thanked us for the unexpected interest we showed in their parents, their childhood and early careers, marveling at how "journalists never asked me these questions." They consider themselves the "Voice" of those who are currently being afflicted, oppressed, and marginalized, and thus their own personal, lived stories fade into the background as they highlight the discrimination and violent oppression faced by the Uyghur community currently living in East Turkestan/Xinjiang.

Our women—"extraordinary" Uyghurs living in the diaspora—provide an intimate, circumscribed perspective on the Xinjiang situation by adding new fragments to a larger, fast expanding mosaic. Their narratives offer vivid glimpses into the "everyday discrimination" that was "normal" for Uyghurs who lived in what they knew as "East Turkestan" before 2017, when the contours of a genocide first became visible to the Western world. Their stories are less dramatic, less shocking than the stories of detainees coming out of the "re-education" camps, but they are of great value for they provide narrative continuity and consistency. They present a narrative of discrimination and marginalization that was clearly present prior to the Strike Hard campaigns and well before the Western world began to hear of the atrocities. In this way, they provide added authority and legitimacy to the claims of those who survived the re-education camps.

These narratives also offer a glimpse into the developments that were occurring in the Uyghur community in the 1990s and 2000s. They provide insight into the daily lives of individuals who were affected by new government policies and initiatives that were intended to disfranchise, decimate, and assimilate the Uyghur people. Their narratives describe experiences of increased checkpoints and surveillance, police harassment and violence, and being led away for questioning. Our subjects tell us how the CCP's policies are applied in real life, often sporadically and inconsistently, so that sometimes they could be evaded or circumvented. These narratives are useful in that they document various stages in the chronological development of a phenomenon which, since 2020, has been widely recognized as a campaign of "genocide." Their stories track the slow tightening of the noose around the Uyghur population of East Turkestan/Xinjiang and provide insight into the pre-existing structural inequality that was in place before the contemporary genocide.

Seven of our subjects left China before the first re-education camps opened (*c.* 2014). They speak of their lived experience, of what happened to them, to their friends, to their relatives living in their cities or villages. At the time, they did not grasp the larger implications of the unpleasant obstacles in their careers; the racism and discrimination they were dealt as students in China's top universities, in the job market, and in the workplace. These narratives reflect the lived Uyghur experience they saw around them. However, despite the "normalcy" of the incidents, they heeded certain warning signals and chose to emigrate. After leaving China, they gained a new political awareness; the direct result of access to the international mass media and to the internet beyond China's "Great Firewall." Exchanging information with fellow Uyghurs in the international diaspora, they enjoyed their new-found right to congregate in groups; a right that was stifled in China. And their lived experiences from China are today being recollected and recounted and freely interpreted.

As previously noted, the personal life stories of these women are generally not part of their campaigns. As human rights advocates, they present speeches, write articles, or plan events that address the broader issues regarding the common plight of the Uyghur people. Thus, their lived experiences, recounted here for the first time, can be viewed and understood as an extension of their activism. Their active retelling of their lived experiences has allowed us to perceive and to make use of their storytelling as a different approach to raising public awareness of the ongoing genocide in Xinjiang.

Notes

Introduction

i   For example, the Uyghur Human Rights Project, and the Uyghur Research Institute.

ii   Rachel Harris, Guangtian Ha, and Maria Jaschok (eds.), *Ethnographies of Islam in China* (Honolulu, HI: University of Hawaii Press, 2020).

iii   See Finley's discussion of the genocide debate: Joanne Smith Finley, "Why Scholars and Activists Increasingly Fear a Uyghur Genocide in Xinjiang," *Journal of Genocide Research* 239, no. 3 (2021), 348–70.

iv   BBC News, "Canada's Parliament Declares China's Treatment of Uighurs 'Genocide,'" February 23, 2021, https://www.bbc.com/news/world-us-canada-56163220

v   Nury Turkel, *No Escape: The True Story of China's Genocide of the Uyghurs* (New York: Hanover Square Press, 2022).

vi   In January 2021 *The New York Times* announced that the State Department declared on Tuesday that the Chinese government is committing genocide and crimes against humanity through its wide-scale repression of Uighurs and other predominantly Muslim ethnic minorities in its northwestern region of Xinjiang, including in its use of internment camps and forced sterilization. The United States State Department recognized the PRC's crimes as genocide, Campaign for Uyghurs refers to "similar resolutions by parliamentary bodies in the United Kingdom, Canada, Czech Republic, Belgium, the Netherlands, France, Lithuania, Ireland, and the European Parliament."

vii   "Adrian Zenz, the Academic behind the 'Xinjiang Police Files,'" *France 24*, May 25, 2022, https://www.france24.com, France 24, Asia/Pacific.

viii   For more information, see Roseanne Gerin, "Belgium, Czech Republic Legislatures Pass Uyghur Genocide Declarations," *Radia Free Asia*, https://www.rfa.org/english/news/uyghur/genocide-declarations-06152021171101.html

ix   The eight governments, so far, that have recognized China's treatment of the Uyghurs as conforming to the criteria of a "genocide" as stated in the 1948 Genocide Convention, are the USA, Canada, the Netherlands, the United Kingdom, Lithuania, the Netherlands, France, Sweden, and the Czech Republic.

x   Uyghur Human Rights Project, "UHRP Welcomes Taiwan's Resolution on Atrocities against Uyghurs," January 3, 2023, https://uhrp.org/statement/uhrp-welcomes-taiwans-resolution-on-atrocities-against-uyghurs/

xi   Nury Turkel, *No Escape: The True Story of China's Genocide of the Uyghurs* (New York: Hanover Square Press, 2022), 32–33.

xii   The four members are Susan J. Palmer, the "Principal Investigator," and three Research Assistants: Marie-Ève Melanson, a Ph.D. candidate in McGill's School of Religious Studies whose field is Religion and Law; Dilmurat Mahmut, a Uyghur student who immigrated to Canada as a skilled immigrant and in 2022 received his Ph.D. in Education from McGill; and Abdulmuqtedir Udun, a Uyghur journalist who writes for the *Uyghur Times* and works as a researcher for Uyghur NGOs.

xiii   I find there is no adequate word for this role that is not clumsy or misleading. The term "human subjects" assures us that they are not guinea pigs or other animals used in experiments. "Informants" sounds very like "informers" or spies—which is how the Chinese police would view our participants. "Research participants" is better, despite its pompous six syllables.

xiv   Some of our Uyghurs refused to meet on Zoom, claiming it was owned by a Chinese millionaire and therefore not secure.

xv   Again, there is not an appropriate word for what these Uyghur women are doing. Several said they disliked being called an "activist", that they were just "raising awareness of the Uyghur genocide and the suffering of our people."

xvi   https://creor-ejournal.library.mcgill.ca/article/view/60

xvii   https://www.hrw.org/report/2021/04/19/break-their-lineage-break-their-roots/chinas-crimes-against-humanity-targeting

xviii   Susan, J. Palmer, Dilmurat Mahmut, Marie-Ève Melanson, and Abdulmuqtedir Udun, The "Uyghurs in the Diaspora in Canada" 2021 Survey Report, McGill University, https://creor-ejournal.library.mcgill.ca/article/view/60

xix   See the interview with Rahima Mahmut in Part Two.

xx   Adrian Zenz uses this term, "social engineering project" to describe the Chinese government's population reduction measures regarding the Uyghur population.

xxi   Since this writing, Gulchehra Hoja and Mihrigul Tursun have each released their memoirs in English: Gulchehra Hoja, A Stone is Most Precious where It Belongs, Oxford, UK: Blackwell's Little, Brown, 2023. Mihrigul Tursun and Andrea C. Hoffman, Place of No Return: How I Survived China's Uyghur Camps. Green Bay, WI: Titletown Publishing, 2023.

Part One: Personal Narratives as an Extension of Uyghur Advocacy Work

i   This research was conducted as one of several initiatives during the *Children in Sectarian Religions and State Control* project at McGill University's School of Religious Studies, a five-year research project supported by Canada's Social Sciences and Humanities Research Council (SSHRC) http//:www. spiritualchildhoods.ca

ii   Adrian Zenz, "Break Their Roots: Evidence for China's Parent–Child Separation Campaign in Xinjiang," *Journal of Political Risk* 7, no. 7 (July 2019), https://www.jpolrisk.com/break-their-roots-evidence-for-chinas-parent-child-separation-campaign-in-xinjiang/#:~:text=Xinjiang%20has%20not%20only%20created,dramatic%20race%20against%20time%20to

iii   The Uyghurs we spoke to routinely refer to Xinjiang province as "East Turkestan" or as "the Homeland."

iv   "The Uyghur Genocide," *Newsline Institute for Strategy and Policy*, March 2021.

v   Sven Spengemann and Peter Fonseca, "The Human Rights Situation of Uyghurs in Xinjiang, China: Report of the Standing Committee on Foreign Affairs and International Development Subcommittee on International Human Rights," House of Commons Canada, March 2021, https://www.ourcommons.ca/Content/Committee/432/FAAE/Reports/RP11164859/sdirrp04/sdirrp04-e.pdf

vi   Valerie J. Janesick, "Oral History Interviewing: Issues and Possibilities," in *The Oxford Handbook of Qualitative Research* (1st ed.), ed. Patricia Leavy (Oxford: Oxford University Press), 300–14, 300, 11.

vii   David King Dunaway, "The Development of Oral History in the United States: The Evolution toward Interdisciplinary," *Revista Tempo E Argumento* 10, no. 24 (2018), 115–35. https://doi.org/10.5965/2175180310242018115

viii   Jakub Mlynář and Jamie Lewis, *Analysing Oral Histories: Social Roles and Narrative Self-Regulation in Holocaust Survivors' Testimonies* (London: SAGE Publications, 2017), https://doi.org/10.4135/9781473999152

ix   Mlynář and Lewis, "Analysing Oral Histories," 2. Emphasis mine.

x   Ibid.

xi   Dunaway, "The Development of Oral History," 125.

xii   Mlynář and Lewis, "Analysing Oral Histories," 3.

xiii   Richard Cándida Smith, "Storytelling as Experience" (Review Essay), *The Oral History Review* 22, no. 2 (Winter 1995), 87–90, 87. Emphasis mine.

xiv   Martin Cortazzi, *Narrative Analysis* (London: Falmer Press, 1993), 2.

xv   See Mlynář and Lewis, "Analysing Oral Histories"; Amia Lieblich, Rivka Tuval-Maschiach, and Tammar Zilber, *Narrative Research: Reading, Analysis and Interpretation* (Thousand Oaks, CA: SAGE, 1998).

xvi   For a sampling of this literature, see: Janesick, "Oral History Interviewing";
          Valerie J. Janesick, "Oral History as a Social Justice Project: Issues for the
          Qualitative Researcher," *The Qualitative Report* 12, no. 1 (2007), 111–21,
          https://doi.org/10.46743/2160-3715/2007.1648; William A. Gamson, "Policy
          Discourse and the Language of the Life-World," in *Eigenwilligkeit und
          Rationalität sozialer Prozesse*, ed. Jurgen Gerhards and Ronald Hitzler (VS
          Verlag für Sozialwissenschaften, 1999), 127–44; William A. Gamson, "How
          Storytelling Can Be Empowering," in *Culture in Mind: Toward a Sociology of
          Culture and Cognition*, ed. Karen Cerulo (New York: Routledge, 2001), 187–
          99; Joseph E. Davis, "Narrative and Social Movements: The Power of Stories,"
          in *Stories of Change: Narratives and Social Movements*, ed. Joseph E. Davis
          (Albany, NY: SUNY, 2002), 3–30; Gary Alan Fine, "The Storied Group: Social
          Movements as 'Bundles of Narratives,'" in *Stories of Change: Narratives and
          Social Movements*, ed. Joseph E. Davis (Albany, NY: SUNY, 2002), 229–46.

xvii   We have chosen to describe the women interviewed as "activists"; however, it
          should be noted that this term is problematic for them. They made the point
          that what they were doing was supporting their brothers and sisters in the
          Homeland as a vital response to an existential crisis, as an urgent duty, not a
          "paid profession." They expressed a wish to distance themselves from what they
          viewed as the glamorous, pretentious role of "activist." However, we have found
          no word in the English or the Uyghur language that adequately describes what
          they do. Therefore, although it might appear to trivialize their endeavors, we
          have chosen to describe them as political or human rights "activists."

xviii   Janesick, "Oral History Interviewing," 303.

xix   Steinar Kvale, *Doing Interviews*. Sage Qualitative Research Kit (London: SAGE
          Publications, 2007), 63–65.

xx   Jo Anne Ollerenshaw and John W. Creswell, "Narrative Research: A
          Comparison of Two Restorying Data Analysis Approaches," *Sage Journals* 8,
          no. 3 (2002), 20.

xxi   Michael Dillon, "Xinjiang before 1949: A Historical Outline," in *Xinjiang:
          China's Muslim Far Northwest* (London: Routledge Curzon, 2004), 9.

xxii   Dillon, "Xinjiang before 1949," 17, 19.

xxiii   Dillon, "Xinjiang before 1949," 20.

xxiv   Dillon, "Xinjiang before 1949," 21.

xxv   Dillon, "Xinjiang before 1949," 22.

xxvi   "Dolkun Isa," n.d., World Uyghur Congress, https://www.uyghurcongress.org/
          en/team/dolkun-isa/

xxvii   Nury Turkel is Chairman of the Board for the Uyghur Human Rights Project
          (UHRP), which he co-founded in 2003. He also served as the President of the
          Uyghur American Association.

xxviii   Ildikó Bellér-Hann, *Community Matters in Xinjiang, 1880–1949: Towards a
          Historical Anthropology of the Uyghurs* (Leiden, Boston, MA: Brill, 2008), 196–200.

xxix   Dilmurat Mahmut and Joanne Smith Finley, "'A man works on the land, a woman works for her man': Building on Jarring's Fascination with Eastern Turki Proverbs," in *Kashgar Revisited: Commemorating the 10th Anniversary of the Death of Ambassador Gunnar Jarring*, ed. Ildikó Bellér-Hann, Birgit N. Schlyter, and June Sugawara (Leiden: Brill, 2017), 302–30.

xxx   Kara Abramson, "Gender, Uyghur Identity, and the Story of Nuzugum," *The Journal of Asian Studies* 71, no. 4 (November 2012), 1071, https://doi.org/10.1017/S002191181200117

xxxi   Abramson, "Gender, Uyghur Identity, and the Story of Nuzugum," 1070.

xxxii   Joanne Smith Finley, "Education, Religion and Identity among Uyghur Hostesses in Ürümchi," in *Language, Education and Uyghur Identity in Urban Xinjiang*, ed. Joanne Smith Finley and Xiaowei Zang (London: Routledge, 2015), 176–93.

xxxiii   Rachel Harris, "The New Battleground: Song-and-dance in China's Muslim Borderlands," *The World of Music* 6, no, 2 (2017), 35–55; James Leibold and Timothy Grose, "Islamic Veiling in Xinjiang: The Political and Societal Struggle to Define Uyghur Female Adornment," *The China Journal* 76 (2016), 78–102.

xxxiv   Rachel Harris, *Soundscapes of Uyghur Islam* (Bloomington, IN: Indiana University Press, 2020).

xxxv   Timothy Grose, "Beautifying Uyghur Bodies: Fashion, 'Modernity', and State Discipline in the Tarim Basin," *Monde chinois* 63 (2020), 12–29.

xxxvi   Sean R. Roberts, *The War on the Uyghurs: China's Internal Campaign against a Muslim Minority* (Princeton, NJ: Princeton University Press, 2020).

xxxvii   Rebiya Kadeer and Alexandra Cavelius, *Dragon Fighter: One Woman's Epic Struggle for Peace with China* (San Diego, CA: Kales Press, 2009); James A. Millward, *Eurasian Crossroads: A History of Xinjiang* (New York: Columbia University Press, 2021).

xxxviii   Darren Byler, "Three Years of Silence: Rahile Dawut Named Honorary Professor," *The China Project*, December 14, 2020; Ruth Ingram, "Where Is Uyghur Folklore Expert Rahile Dawut?," *The Diplomat*, November 23, 2020.

xxxix   https://opensocietyuniversitynetwork.org/newsroom/uyghur-scholar-rahile-dawut-named-first-osun-honorary-professor-in-the-humanities-2020-12-08

xl   https://thediplomat.com/2020/11/where-is-uyghur-folklore-expert-rahile-dawut/

xli   We found that young Uyghur second-generation activists in the West freely admit they are "feminists."

xlii   Interview with Kabir Qurban, March 29, 2022.

xliii   Interview with Mihrigul Tursun on December 7, 2021.

xliv   Omir Bekali was detained from March to November 2017 and complained of torture, solitary confinement, indoctrination, of being forced to sign a confession, and to eat pork and drink alcohol. See Gerry Shih and Dake Kang, "Muslims Forced to Drink Alcohol and Eat Pork in China's 'Re-Education' Camps, Former Inmate Claims," *The Independent*, May 18, 2018.

xlv   Matthew Hill, David Campanale, and Joel Gunter, "'Their Goal Is to Destroy Everyone': Uighur Camp Detainees Allege Systematic Rape," BBC News, February 2, 2021.

xlvi   Interview with Zumretay Arkin on March 14, 2022.

xlvii Nury Turkel, *No Escape: The True Story of China's Genocide of the Uyghurs* (New York: Hanover Square Press, 2022).

xlviii Adrian Zenz, "Sterilizations, IUDs, and Mandatory Birth Control: The CCP's Campaign to Suppress Uyghur Birthrates in Xinjiang," *Victims of Communism*, June 29, 2020.

xlix   "Once Oppressed, Xinjiang's Uyghur Women Take on Chinese Government," *ANI News*, March 14, 2021.

l   Timothy Grose, "Beautifying Uyghur bodies: Fashion, Modernity and State Power in the Tarim Basin," *The Contemporary China Centre Blog*, University of Westminster, October 12, 2019, https://blog.westminster.ac.uk/contemporarychina/beautifying-uyghur-bodies-fashion-modernity-and-state-power-in-the-tarim-basin-2/

li   Ibid.

lii   Rebiya Kadeer and Alexandra Cavelius, *Dragon Fighter: One Woman's Epic Struggle or Peace with China* (San Diego, CA: Kales Press, 2009).

liii   Interview with Mihrigul Tursun on December 7, 2021.

liv   Cindy Huang, "Muslim Women at a Crossroads: Gender and Development in the Xinjiang Uyghur Autonomous Region, China," Ph.D. dissertation (University of California, Berkeley, 2009).

lv   Cindy Huang, "Muslim Women at a Crossroad," vi.

lvi   Rosemary Radford Ruether, *Sexism and God Talk: Towards a Feminist Theology* (Boston, MA: Beacon Press, 1993), 106–07.

lvii   Zubayra Shamseden, "I Have Revised My Idea of What a Uighur Heroine Should Be," *ChinaFile*, April 19, 2019, https://www.chinafile.com/reporting-opinion/viewpoint/i-have-revised-my-idea-of-what-uighur-heroine-should-be

lviii Saba Mahmood, *Politics of Piety: The Islamic Revival and the Feminist Subject* (Princeton, NJ: Princeton University Press, 2012).

Part Two: The Narratives

i   Zumrat Dawut's story can be found in this *Insider* cartoon by artist Fahmida Azim, https://www.insider.com/comic-i-escaped-a-chinese-internment-camp-uyghur-2021-12; Mihrigul Tursun's story is told in this Japanese manga comic, https://share.america.gov/japanese-manga-comic-tells-story-of-uyghur-oppression/

ii   Ghulja is a special place, in that it is the birthplace of second East Turkestan republic. It has been dubbed the "Rebel City" and has been a politically sensitive area through the CCP's repressive politics.

iii   Zubayra Shamseden has written many articles and given interviews on the Ghulja Massacre of 1997 and on the Uyghur genocide, https://thediplomat.com/2021/02/the-ghulja-massacre-of-1997-and-the-face-of-uyghur-genocide-today/ https://www.chinafile.com/reporting-opinion/viewpoint/i-have-revised-my-idea-of-what-uighur-heroine-should-be https://bitterwinter.org/uyghurs-are-forced-to-denounce-their-faith-to-survive/ https://hongkongfp.com/2020/02/07/ghulja-massacre-remembering-chinas-brutal-crackdown-peaceful-xinjiang-protest/ https://globalengage.org/person/zubayra-shamseden/fellows https://www.worldpoliticsreview.com/trend-lines/25898/china-s-uighur-crackdown-is-turning-xinjiang-into-a-police-state

iv   When Palmer expressed surprise during the interview with Zubayra, the latter and the two Uyghur RAs explained that this was quite common in China; that companies behaved as if they owned their employees, and to resign was viewed as a betrayal that demanded compensation.

v   The *meshreps* were inspirational gatherings that involved singing, dancing, feasting, inspirational religious speeches. They were often concluded with a soccer game.

vi   For a detailed account of this incident, read Palmer and Udun, https://ottawacitizen.com/opinion/palmer-and-udun-beijing-olympics-where-are-the-uyghur-athletes

vii   Rukiye Turdush also noted that her blog becomes empty every two weeks, and she suspects that the CCP is doing this. She has had to ask the site owner to restore her content. Her provider claims they don't know what is happening to her blog.

viii   https://thediplomat.com/2017/06/i-am-uyghur-and-i-will-protest/

ix   This interview was conducted in English since Zubayra speaks English impeccably. She is a Muslim, but chose the word "God" rather than "Allah."

x   Dolkun Isa began his work as an activist as a student-leader at Xinjiang University. After leading pro-democracy student demonstrations in 1988, he was dismissed from university and endured years of persecution by the Chinese government, finally fleeing China in 1994 and seeking asylum in Europe. He became a German citizen in 2006. In 1996, Isa helped establish the World Uyghur Youth Congress. In 2004, he helped found the World Uyghur Congress (WUC). Isa was elected WUC president in 2017.

xi   Rukiye Turdush has authored the following books: *Yearning for Freedom* (Istanbul: Teklimakan Publishing, 2017)(in Uyghur); *Ethnicity, Nation, Nationalism and Identity* (Istanbul: Uyghur Research Institute, 2019) (in Uyghur); *East Turkistan's Right to Sovereignty: Decolonization and Beyond* (Lexington Books, 2022) (in English).

xii   For more information see Gardner Bovingdon, *The Uyghurs: Strangers in Their Own Land* (New York: Columbia University, 2010).

xiii Uyghurs generally do not want to be recognized as Chinese. Smith Finley (2013) sees this phenomenon as "symbolic resistance" to Chinese oppression and discrimination.

xiv   The notion that "Xinjiang has always been an inseparable part of China," has long been held by the CCP who have produced a white paper on this. Alternative views are condemned as separatism which leads to serious legal prosecutions. (See Xinhua, "White Paper: Xinjiang Inseparable Part of China." *China Daily Hong Kong*, July 21 2019, https://www.chinadailyhk. com/articles/228/219/155/1563683130475.html#:~:text=Xinjiang%20has%20 long%20been%20an).

xv   For more information, see Ian W. Campbell, "'Our Friendly Rivals': Rethinking the Great Game in Ya'qub Beg's Kashgaria, 1867–77," *Central Asian Survey* 33, no. 2 (2014), 199–214, https://doi.org/10.1080/02634937.20 14.915613

xvi   There is no way of verifying these comments by Rukiye's grandmother, which may seem to feed into the racist trope that "Chinese people will eat anything." However, to frame these comments as a form of "reverse racism" (racism from a repressed minority towards the oppressing majority) would be misguided. As noted by literary critic and legal scholar Stanley Eugene Fish, although oppressed minorities and oppressing majorities may both possess "a ready store of dismissive epithets, ridiculing stories, self-serving folk-myths, and expressions of plain hatred, all directed at the other community [...] it would be bizarre to regard their respective racisms—if that is the word—as equivalent," as "there is certainly a distinction to be made between the ideological hostility of the oppressor and the experience-based hostility of those who have been oppressed." See Stanley Eugene Fish, *There's No Such Thing as Free Speech, and It's a Good Thing, Too* (New York: Oxford University Press, 1994).

xvii For further information on the Xianjiang's Production and Construction Corps see: James D. Seymour, "Xinjiang's Production and Construction Corps, and the Sinification of Eastern Turkestan," *Inner Asia* 2, no. 2 (2000), 171–93, http://www.jstor.org/stable/23615556

xviii On February 5, 1997, hundreds of Uyghur youth took to the streets of Ghulja protesting the unjust policies of the government regarding the Uyghurs. The peaceful demonstration was brutally suppressed by the government. The main reason behind the protest was believed to be the prohibition of Uyghur social organizations known as *mäshräp*. *Mäshräp* actually has been part of Uyghur culture for many centuries. Traditionally, *mäshräp* gatherings were attended by Uyghur men and would involve musical performances, teaching Islamic codes of conduct, and telling jokes. As it was Islamic in nature, no drinking would be allowed. From 1994, Uyghurs in Ghulja started to revive this tradition in order to combat alcoholism and drug abuse growing among Uyghur youth. Soon, a soccer tournament was added to such gatherings. In 1996, the Chinese government began to crack down on *mäshräp* gatherings. For more information, see James A. Millward, "Violent Separatism in Xinjiang: A Critical Assessment," *Policy Studies 6* (Washington, D.C.: East–West Center, 2004), https://www.eastwestcenter.org/system/tdf/private/PS006.pdf?file=1&type=node&id=32006

xix   For more information on Rukiye's Twitter account visit RukiyeTurdush@parlabest, https://twitter.com/parlabest?ref_src=twsrc%5Egoogle%7Ctwcamp%5Eserp%7Ctwgr%5Eauthor

xx   Coletta Amanda, "Canada's 'Two Michaels' Back Home after More than 1,000 Days Imprisoned in China as Huawei's Meng Cuts Deal with U.S," *Washington Post*, September 25, 2021, https://www.washingtonpost.com/world/2021/09/24/canada-two-michaels-china-huawei/

xxi   For example, see Rukiye Turdush and Magnus Fiskesjö, "Dossier: Uyghur Women in China's Genocide," *Genocide Studies and Prevention: An International Journal* 15, no. 1 (2021), 22–43, https://doi.org/10.5038/1911-9933.15.1.1834; Rukiye Turdush, "Why Canada Should Take the Lead in Recognizing China's Crimes against Uyghurs as Genocide," *Medium*, September 23, 2020, https://medium.com/@rukiyeturdush/why-canada-should-take-the-lead-in-recognizing-chinas-crimes-against-uyghurs-as-genocide-df11d386e5bd

xxii   Huseyin Celil is a Uyghur Canadian who has been living in a Chinese prison since 2006, on charges of teaching the language, faith, and culture of the Uyghurs. For more information, see Chris MacLeod, "Huseyin Celil Is the Forgotten Canadian Detained in China," *Toronto Star*, March 15, 2021, https://www.thestar.com/opinion/contributors/2021/03/15/huseyin-celil-is-the-forgotten-canadian-detained-in-china.html

xxiii   See Adam Carter, "Activist Accuses Chinese Government of Meddling after McMaster Speech Disrupted," *CBC News*, February 15, 2019, https://www.cbc.ca/news/canada/hamilton/mcmaster-university-china-1.5021406

xxiv   See Timothy Grose, *Negotiating Inseparability in China: The Xinjiang Class and the Dynamics of Uyghur Identity* (Hong Kong: Hong Kong University Press, 2019).

xxv   This story resonates with Schein's notion of the discourse of "Internal Orientalism" (Schein, 1997: 89) in which China's minorities, especially the Uyghurs, are categorized as "female, rural, and backward," while the majority modern "Han urbanite" as the paradigms of "progress." See Louisa Schein, "Gender and Internal Orientalism in China," *Modern China* 23, no. 1 (January 1997), 69–98, https://doi.org/10.1177/009770049702300103

xxvi This is still a controversial issue, sometimes dismissed as a conspiracy theory. See David Matas and David Kilgour, *Bloody Harvest: Organ Harvesting of Falun Gong Practitioners in China* (Woodstock, ON, Canada: Seraphim Editions, 2009). See also, Ethan Guttman, *The Slaughter: Mass Killings, Organ Harvesting, and China's Secret Solution to Its Dissident Problem* (New York: Prometheus Books, 2014).

xxvii This is also highly controversial and only reported in media outlets. See Keoni Everington, "Saudis Allegedly Buy 'Halal Organs' from 'Slaughtered' Xianjiang Muslims," *Taiwan News*, January 22, 2020, https://www.taiwannews.com.tw/en/news/386257; Adam Withnall, "China is Killing Religious and Ethnic Minorities and Harvesting their Organs, UN Human Rights Council Told," *Independent*, September 24, 2019, https://www.independent.co.uk/news/world/asia/china-religious-ethnic-minorities-uighur-muslim-harvest-organs-un-human-rights-a9117911.html

xxviii This reminds us of a news report mentioning the existence of a priority lane labeled as special passengers/human organs transport lane in Kashgar Airport (Cheung, 2019).

xxix Uyghur students who attended Chinese schools are called *minkaohan* in Chinese, which refers to minority students receiving Chinese medium education. For more information on the education in Xinjiang, see J. Smith Finley, "'Ethnic Anomaly' or Modern Uyghur Survivor? A Case Study of the Minkaohan Hybrid Identity in Xinjiang," in *Situating the Uyghurs between China and Central Asia*, ed. I. Bellér-Hann, M. C. Cesàro, R. Harris, and J. Smith Finley (Aldershot: Ashgate, 2007), 219–37.

xxx   For more information on such oppressive policies, see Bovingdon, *The Uyghurs: Strangers in Their Own Land*; S. R. Roberts, *The War on the Uyghurs: China's Internal Campaign against a Muslim Minority* (Princeton, NJ: Princeton University Press, 2020).

xxxi There exists a strong discrimination in academia as well as popular discourses that minority ethnic groups, including Uyghurs are backward and under-civilized, so they should follow the guidance of Han Chinese in order to reach prosperity. For more information, see L. Schein, "Gender and internal orientalism in China," in *Modern China* 23, no. 1 (1997), 69–98.

xxxii Uyghurs are regarded by Chinese as thieves, potential criminals, or simply people with bad characters or behaviors. For more information, see N.

Baranovitch, "From the Margins to the Centre: The Uyghur Challenge in Beijing," *China Quarterly* 175(2003), 726–50; Raphael Israeli, "China's Uyghur Problem," *Israel Journal of Foreign Affairs*, 4, no. 1 (2010), 89–101.

xxxiii   Although, one of the main purposes of "bilingual" education is to better prepare Uyghur graduates for employment by effectively improving their Chinese language skills, the reality shows that the Uyghur graduates who have obtained full Chinese proficiency would still become the victims of discrimination in the job market (Howell, 2013; Simayi, 2015). For example, according to Zang's study (2011) the Uyghurs earned around 30 percent less than Han Chinese in Ürümqi, the capital city of Xinjiang, in 2011. It is also estimated that overall employment rate of Uyghur graduates around 2013 dropped to as low as 15 percent (Tohti, 2013).

xxxiv   On February 5, 1997, hundreds of Uyghur youth took to the streets of Ghulja protesting the unjust actions of government police forces towards Uyghurs. The peaceful demonstration was brutally suppressed by the government. The main reason behind the protest was believed to be the prohibition of Uyghur social organizations known as *mäshräp*. For further discussion of the Ghulja Incident of 1997 see Rebiya Kadeer, "Fighting for Uyghur Rights," *American Journal of Islamic Social Sciences* 23, no. 3 (2006), 144–48; Peter Irwin, "Remembering the Ghulja Incident: 20th Anniversary of 'Uyghur Tiananmen' Passes with Little Notice," *The Diplomat*, March 2, 2017, https://thediplomat.com/2017/03/remembering-the-ghulja-incident-20th-anniversary-of-uyghur-tiananmen-passes-with-little-notice/; Zubayra Shamseden, "The Ghulja Massacre of 1997 and the Face of Uyghur Genocide Today," *The Diplomat*, February 5, 2021, https://thediplomat.com/2021/02/the-ghulja-massacre-of-1997-and-the-face-of-uyghur-genocide-today/

xxxv   This has been a widespread practice in inner Chinese cities. Tibetans also face such discrimination and exclusion. For more information, see G. A. Bunin, "'We're a People Destroyed': Why Uighur Muslims across China are Living in Fear," *The Guardian* (2018, August 7), https://www.theguardian.com/news/2018/aug/07/why-uighur-muslims-across-china-are-living-in-fear

xxxvi   For a detailed description of the high level of surveillance in China, see Darren Byler, *In the Camps: Life in China's High-Tech Penal Colony* (New York: Penguin Books, 2021).

xxxvii   With the 2016 appointment of Chen Quanguo, the former Party Secretary in Tibet, to the position of secretary of the CCP in the Xinjiang Uygur Autonomous Region, the communication between the Uyghurs in Xinjiang and relatives abroad started to be strictly controlled. By the end of 2016, most Uyghurs lost their contact with their family members in Xinjiang. For more information, see https://www.hrw.org/report/2018/09/09/eradicating-ideological-viruses/chinas-campaign-repression-against-xinjiangs

xxxviii   Some of the media coverage pertaining to Raziya Mahmut is listed here:
           https://ici.radio-canada.ca/nouvelle/1404292/chine-surveillance-minorite-
           ouigoure-canada; https://www.iheartradio.ca/580-cfra/podcasts/listen-now-
           this-uighur-woman-exiled-in-canada-fears-for-her-family-and-community-in-
           china-facing-alleged-genocide-amid-covid-19-1.13409516; https://www.msn.
           com/fr-ca/sports/plus-de-sports/le-cri-d-alarme-de-la-communauté-ouïgoure-
           au-monde-olympique/ar-BB1dbgbJ; https://www.bnaibrith.ca/lets-demand-
           justice-for-the-uyghur-people/

xxxix   Raziya became emotional several times during our interview. For her, she said,
           this has become "normal."

xl   https://foreignpolicy.com/2020/05/28/hong-kong-nationalism-china-security-
           law-protests/

xli   https://www.forbes.com/sites/wadeshepard/2020/01/29/how-chinas-belt-and-
           road-became-a-global-trail-of-trouble/?sh=58e54ac4443d

xlii   Timothy A. Grose, "The Xinjiang Class: Education, Integration, and the
           Uyghurs," *Journal of Muslim Minority Affairs* 30, no. 1 (March 2010), 97–109.

xliii   The Xinjiang Ban required that every year the CCP chose 1,000 children from
           different villages, 14-15-year-olds. Later they raised the number to 3,880
           children. By 2021 it was 5,000. The children would be placed in a Mainland
           China school where they would be raised like the Han Chinese children until
           they finished middle school.

xliv   Quoted in Jay Nordlinger, in "Be a Human." *National Review Plus*, May 17, 2021.

xlv   Gulchehra Hoja (January 30, 2018), "I Lost All Hope of Surviving," *Radio Free
           Asia.*

xlvi   Nordlinger, 2021.

xlvii   Ibid.

xlviii   "Radio Free Asia Uyghur Journalist Wins Magnitsky Human Rights Award,"
           United States Agency for Global Media, November 15, 2019.

xlix   *The 500 Most Influential Muslims* (archived from the original on October 13,
           2020).

l   https://www.rfa.org/english/news/uyghur/hair-05282020155504.
           html?searchterm:utf8:ustring=%20xinjiang%20hair

li   Gardner Bovingdon, *The Uyghurs: Strangers in Their Own Land* (New York:
           Columbia University Press, 2010).

lii   Many of Gulchehra Hoja's academic papers can be found on her Academia
           page: https://inalco.academia.edu/DilnurReyhan; Dilnur Reyhan, "Les
           Ouïghours en Syrie: Mythes, suppositions, et réalités fragmentaires," *Revue
           du monde musulman et de la Méditerranée* 145(2019 209201), 257–79, https://
           doi.org/10.4000/remmm.12422; (Interview) 2019. Dilnur Reyhan: "La
           transmission de la culture ouïghoure fait partie du combat politique," https://
           asialyst.com/fr/2019/03/26/xinjiang-dilnur-reyhan-transmission-culture-

ouighour-partie-combat-politique-chine/; (Interview) 2019. La quête d'équité d'une femme ouïghoure: Entretien avec Dilnur Reyhan, https://www.actualite-news.com/fr/international/europe/turquie/29738-la-quete-d-equite-d-une-femme-ouighoure-entretien-avec-dilnur-reyhan; (Interview) 2020. Dilnur Reyhan: "Confinement ou pas, le bulldozer chinois continue d'éradiquer les Ouïghours," https://www.franceculture.fr/geopolitique/dilnur-reyhan-confinement-ou-pas-le-bulldozer-chinois-continue-deradiquer-les-ouighours; (Interview) 2020. "Dilnur Reyhan, défenseuse des droits des Ouïghour·e·s, déplore l'absence de solidarité entre musulman·e·s," https://fr.globalvoices.org/2020/05/30/251385/

liii   Zumrat had been summoned by the Scientific Development District Street Committee in Urumqi, and she was interned in what local residents call Bei Zan Prison, the so-called Scientific Development District Re-education Centre. This facility is one of many where China's authorities have held up to 1.5 million Uyghurs and other Muslim ethnic minorities accused since April 2017, https://www.rfa.org/english/news/uyghur/interview-inmate-09242019174449.html

liv   Abduhelil claimed he had told Zumrat "to stop spreading rumors and retract the lies she peddled online previously. She cried and said yes. But later, she continued peddling lies online." Liu Xin and Fan Lingzhi, "GT Reporters' Visits Unveil Facts about Xinjiang," *Global Times*, November 17, 2019.

lv   Ibid.

lvi   The Chinese government initially changed the Uyghur alphabet into the Russian alphabet. After their relationship deteriorated with the Soviet Union, they changed it back to the Uyghur alphabet, and then to the Latin alphabet for some years, and then back to the original Uyghur alphabet. For this reason, there is a generation of Uyghur, like Mihrigul's father, who cannot write using the Uyghur alphabet.

lvii   This was the famous footage filmed from a balcony overlooking the square where the Uyghurs were beaten to death by Han Chinese workers wielding clubs. This video went "viral" and triggered the protest in Urumqi on July 5, 2009.

lviii   https://hongkongfp.com/2018/12/08/video-full-ex-xinjiang-detainee-mihrigul-tursuns-full-testimony-us-congressional-hearing/

lix   It might be conjectured that these pivotal experiences or turning points led Mihrigul to what William James would call a "conversion experience." Her father was a devout Muslim, but since the age of 11, Mihrigul had received a strictly secular her education in Chinese institutions. But after moving to Egypt, she married an Egyptian Muslim in a *Nikah* ceremony who taught her the *Qur'an*, and while she was suffering in Chinese prisons it appears she revisited her Muslim faith.

lx   *Ort ohne Wiederkehr* (*Place Without Return*), co-authored with German journalist Andrea Hoffmann.

Part Three: Restoring a Genocide

i   Genevieve Boast, *Tough Bliss: Restorying Life* (Createspace Independent Publishing Platform, 2018).

ii   Mary DeMocker, *The Parents' Guide to Climate Revolution* (New World Library: Novato, California, 2018).

iii   K. Suddaby, J. Landau, "Positive and Negative Timelines: A Technique for Restorying," *Fam Process* 37, no. 3 (1998, Fall), 287–98.

iv   "FAQs: Truth and Reconciliation Commission," *CBC News*, retrieved March 15, 2018, https://www.cbc.ca/aboriginal/truth-reconciliation/

v   Darren Byler, *In the Camps: China's High-Tech Penal Colony* (New York: Random House, 2021).

vi   John Kleinig, "Whistleblower," in *The Encyclopedia of Governance*, ed. Mark Brevil (New York: SAGE, 2006).

vii   The Uyghur Tribunal was an independent "people's tribunal" based in the United Kingdom that aims to examine evidence regarding China's ongoing human rights abuses against the Uyghur people and to evaluate whether the abuses constitute genocide under the Genocide Convention. The tribunal was chaired by Geoffrey Nice, the lead prosecutor in the trial of Slobodan Milošević, who announced the creation of the tribunal in September 2020.

viii   Timothy Grose, *Negotiating Inseparability in China: The Xinjiang Class and the Dynamics of Uyghur Identity* (Hong Kong: Hong Kong University Press, 2019).

ix   Ibid.

x   One example is Rushan Abbas' use of the documentary film, "In Search of My Sister" to protest and broadcast her sister's disappearance.

xi   A similar cartoon was made of Zumrat Dawat's story (https://table.media/china/en/feature/comic-reportage-how-zumrat-dawut-escaped-from-a-camp-in-xinjiang/).

xii   https://www.reuters.com/article/us-japan-uighur-comic-idUKKBN1YV0QC

xiii   https://www.nytimes.com/2009/05/28/world/asia/28kashgar.html

xiv   https://www.hrw.org/report/2021/04/19/break-their-lineage-break-their-roots/chinas-crimes-against-humanity-targeting

xv   https://www.theatlantic.com/international/archive/2018/09/china-internment-camps-muslim-uighurs-satellite/569878/

xvi   Sigal Samuel, "Internet Sleuths Are Hunting for China's Secret Internment Camps for Muslims," *The Atlantic*, September 10, 2018.

xvii   Nury Turkel, *No Escape* (Toronto: Hanover Square Press, 2022), 88.

xviii   https://www.theguardian.com/commentisfree/2020/sep/24/china-imprisoning-uighurs-satellite-images-xinjiang

xix https://www.theglobeandmail.com/world/article-china-detaining-hundreds-
     of-thousands-of-uyghurs-in-prison-like/
xx   Interview with Darren Byler, March 16, 2021.
xxi Gilles Sabrié, "Beijing Has Sought for Decades to Suppress Uighur Resistance
     to Chinese Rule in Xinjiang," *The New York Times*, November 16, 2019;
     Adrian Zenz, "Sterilizations, IUDs, and Mandatory Birth Control: The
     CCP's Campaign to Suppress Uyghur Birthrates in Xinjiang," *The Jamestown
     Foundation*, June 2020.
xxii Adrian Zenz, "The Karakax List: Dissecting the Anatomy of Beijing's
     Internment Drive in Xinjiangm," *Journal of Political Risk* 8, no. 2 (February
     2020), https://victimsofcommunism.org/publication/karakax-list-dissecting-
     anatomy-beijings-internment-drive-xinjiang/
xxiii Zenz notes, "Recently, population in the PRC (to include Xinjiang) has been
     counted in two different ways. The first is 'household registered population'
     (年末户籍人口, nianmo huji renkou) which refers to people who are formally
     registered as being from Xinjiang under China's household registration, or
     'hukou' (户口) system. The second is 'permanent resident population' (年末总
     人口, nianmo zong renkou—or—年末常住人口, nianmo changzhu renkou)
     which refers to the number of people locally residing in Xinjiang by December
     31of each respective year, who have lived in there for at least 6 months" (National
     Bureau of Statistics, October12, 2018; Macroeconomic Situation, June 2009).
xxiv Timothy A. Grose, "Chinese Social Media Sources Leave No Room for Denial:
     Documenting Human Rights Violations in Xinjiang," *Journal of Ethnographic
     Theory* 12, no. 2 (2002), 392–404.
xxv Ibid.
xxvi "Adrian Zenz, the Academic behind the 'Xinjiang Police Files,'" *France 24*,
     May 25, 2022.
xxvii https://www.france24.com/en/asia-pacific/20220525-adrian-zenz-the-
     academic-behind-the-xinjiang-police-files-on-china-s-abuse-of-uighurs
xxviii Adrian Zenz, "The Xinjiang Police Files: Re-Education Camp Security and
     Political Paranoia in the Xinjiang Uyghur Autonomous Region," *The Journal of
     the European Association for Chinese Studies* 3 (2022), 1–56.
xxix "Adrian Zenz, the Academic Behind the 'Xinjiang Police Files,'" *France 24*,
     May 25, 2022.
xxx https://ge.usembassy.gov/uyghur-authors-detail-abuses-in-their-homeland/
xxxi ttps://www.brookings.edu/wp-content/uploads/2020/09/FP_20200914_china_
     oppression_xinjiang_millward_peterson.pdf; Maya Wang, "'Eradicating
     Ideological Viruses'" (New York: Human Rights Watch, September 9, 2018),
     https://www.hrw.org/report/2018/09/09/eradicating-ideological-viruses/
     chinas-campaign-repressionagainst-xinjiangs; "China Cuts Uighur Births with

IUDs, Abortion, Sterilization," Associated Press; Adrian Zenz, "Sterilizations, IUDs, and Mandatory Birth Control."

xxxii Lucas Niewenhuis, "China's 'Social Re-Engineering' of Uyghurs, Explained by Darren Byler," The China Project, August 15, 2019, https://signal.supchina. com/chinas-social-re-engineering-of-uyghurs-explained-by-darren-byler/

xxxiii https://www.cbc.ca/news/world/china-internment-camps-1.4666686

xxxiv Notably, the accounts of Mihrigul Tursun, Gulbahar Jalilova, Zumrat Dawat, Sayragul Sawutbay and Tursunay Ziyawudun.

xxxv James Millward, "China's Fruitless Repression of the Uighurs," op-ed, *The New York Times*, p. A27, September 29, 2014.

xxxvi Darren Byler is a lecturer in the Department of Anthropology at the University of Washington. He speaks Uyghur and has researched Uyghur culture and writes the Xinjiang Column for *SupChina*; Dr. Adrian Zenz is a German anthropologist, the author of *Tibetanness under Threat* and co-editor of *Mapping Amdo: Dynamics of Change*.

xxxvii James A. Millward is a professor in the Department of History at Georgetown University.

xxxviii https://www.nytimes.com/2014/09/29/opinion/chinas-fruitless-repression-of-the-uighurs.html

xxxix Connor W. Dooley, "Silencing Xinjiang: The Chinese Government's Campaign againt the Uyghurs"; J. D. Candidate, University of Georgia School of Law, 2020. B.A., Southern Methodist University, 2017: 247.

xl Jelil Kashgary et al., "China Steps up 'Strike Hard' Campaign in Xinjiang," (Luisetta Mudie trans.), January 9, 2014.

xli Dooley, 2017: 262.

xlii The Belt and Road is a massive infrastructure project that focuses on pipelines, highways, and railways on the Silk Road that is projected to expand from East Asia to Europe to connect China with these countries.

xliii Sigal Samuel, "Internet Sleuths are Hunting for China's Secret Internment Camps for Muslims: The Country Is Using High-Tech Methods of Repression, but Even the Simplest Tech May Be Enough to Expose Them," *The Atlantic*, September 15, 2018.

xliv https://www.theglobeandmail.com/world/article-china-detaining-hundreds-of-thousands-of-uyghurs-in-prison-like/

xlv Interview with Darren Byler, November 16, 2021.

xlvi David A. Millward, "China's system of oppression in Xinjiang," Brookings, 2020.

xlvii https:// www.brookings.edu/wp-content/uploads/2020/09/FP_20200914_china_oppression_xinjiang_millward_peterson

xlviii   Sean R. Roberts, *The War on the Uyghurs: China's Internal Campaign against a Muslim Minority* (Princeton, NJ: Princeton University Press, 2020).

xlix   David Tobin, *Securing China's Northwest Frontier: Identity and Insecurity in Xinjiang* (Cambridge: Cambridge University Press, 2020), 58, 225.

l   Adrian Zenz, "The Xinjiang Police Files: Re-Education Camp Security and Political Paranoia in the Xinjiang Uyghur Autonomous Region," *The Journal of the European Association for Chinese Studies* 3 (December 2022), 263–311.

li   Tobin, 2020.

lii   Lee and Yazici Greitens, 2020

liii   Dirk A. Moses, "Paranoia and Partisanship: Genocide Studies, Holocaust Historiography, and the 'Apolitical Conjuncture,'" *The Historical Journal* 54, no. 2 (2011), 576.

liv   Robert S. Robins and Jerrod M. Post, *Political Paranoia: The Psychopolitics of Hatred* (New Haven, CT: Yale University Press, 1997).

lv   Zenz, "The Xinjiang Police Files: Re-Education Camp Security and Political Paranoia in the Xinjiang Uyghur Autonomous Region."

lvi   Humeyra Pamuk and David Brunnstrom, "U.S. Leads Condemnation of China for 'horrific' Repression of Muslims," September 24, 2019, Reuters.

lvii   https://globalnews.ca/video/7674308/chinese-ambassador-calls-uighurs-genocide-allegations-lies-of-the-century

lviii   https://www.mfa.gov.cn/ce/cgtrt//eng/news/t1874254.htm

lix   https://www.courthousenews.com/netherlands-lashes-out-against-genocide-of-uighur-people-in-china/

lx   Humeyra Pamuk, "Pompeo Says U.S. Troubled by Reports of China Harassing Families of Uighur Activists," Reuters, November 5, 2019, https://www.reuters.com/article/us-usa-china-muslims-pompeo-idUSKBN1XF20S

lxi   https://foreignpolicy.com/2020/07/01/china-documents-uighur-genocidal-sterilization-xinjiang/

lxii   "US Voices Disgust at China Boast of Uighur Population Control," Arab News, January 9, 2021.

lxiii   Lian Yuchun, Li Yuanbin and Li Dabiao, "Xinjiang Think Tank Unveils Adrian Zenz as Swindler under Academic Disguise," *The Global Times*, August 9, 2020.

lxiv   https://campaignforuyghurs.org/cfu-condemns-spokesperson-of-the-peoples-government-of-xuars-response-to-the-xinjiang-police-files/

lxv   Zenz pointed out that Anayat did not challenge the authenticity of Xinjiang Police Files per se, but rather attacked Zenz's *interpretation* of the files. Zenz notes, "This implies that the files were in fact derived from 'Xinjiang police' computers and indirectly confirms that the files depict actual Uyghur people. It just shows the significance of this type of evidence, which the Chinese state finds very difficult to refute, also … the fact that there is so much material, so much visual and image material … makes it basically impossible to refute its authenticity," https://campaignforuyghurs.org/cfu-condemns-spokesperson-of-the-peoples-government-of-xuars-response-to-the-xinjiang-police-files/

lxvi   https://www.youtube.com/watch?v=rsQxjFCh5zU

lxvii   https://www.globaltimes.cn/page/201911/1170249.shtml

lxviii https://www.theatlantic.com/international/archive/2018/09/china-internment-camps-muslim-uighurs-satellite/569878/

lxix   Timothy Grose is an Associate Professor of China Studies at Rose-Hulman Institute of Technology in Indiana.

lxx   https://www.theatlantic.com/international/archive/2018/09/china-internment-camps-muslim-uighurs-satellite/569878/

lxxi   https://www.bushcenter.org/publications/chinas-persecution-of-uyghur-muslims-is-an-attack-on-freedom-and-democracy

lxxii   https://www.bushcenter.org/publications/chinas-persecution-of-uyghur-muslims-is-an-attack-on-freedom-and-democracy

lxxiii https://www.bushcenter.org/publications/chinas-persecution-of-uyghur-muslims-is-an-attack-on-freedom-and-democracy

lxxiv   Interview with Gulchehra Hoja, May 1, 2021.

lxxv   https://theconversation.com/how-an-independent-tribunal-came-to-rule-that-china-is-guilty-of-genocide-against-the-uyghurs-173604

lxxvi   "Why Can 'Uyghur Tribunal' Farce Be Staged in the West?," *The Global Times*, December 11, 2021.

lxxvii Liu Xin, "Staging Farce Shows No Respect to True Terror Victims," *The Global Times,* September 9, 2021.

lxxviii Amia Lieblich, Rivka Tuval-Maschiach, and Tammar Zilber, *Narrative Research: Reading, Analysis and Interpretation* (Thousand Oaks, CA: SAGE, 1998).

lxxix   J. Clausen, "Life Reviews and Life Stories," *Methods of Life Course Research*, ed. J. Giele and G. Elder (New York: SAGE Publications, 1998), 189–212, 190.

lxxx   Jerome Bruner, "The Narrative Creation of Self," *The Handbook of Narrative and Psychotherapy*, ed. Lynne E. Angus and John McLeod (Thousand Oaks, CA: SAGE Publications, 2004), 21.

lxxxi   Dan P. McAdams and Philip J. Bowman, "Narrating Life's Turning Points: Redemption and Contamination," in *Turns in the Road: Narrative Studies of Lives in Transition*, ed. D. P. McAdams, R. Josselson, and A. Lieblich (Washington, D.C.: American Psychological Association, 2001), 5.

lxxxii McAdams and Bowman, "Narrating Life's Turning Points," 5.

lxxxiii Ibid.

lxxxiv Kenneth J. Gergen and Mary M. Gergen, "Narrative and the Self as Relationship," in *Advances in Experimental Social Psychology, Volume Twenty-One*, ed. Leonard Berkowitz (San Diego, CA: Academic Press, 1988), 24.

lxxxv   Ibid.

lxxxvi   Rukiye Turdush and Magnus Fiskesjö, "Dossier: Uyghur Women in China's
         Genocide," *Genocide Studies and Prevention: An International Journal* 15, no. 1
         (2021), 22–43.

lxxxvii Daniel Haitas, "Shang Yang and Legalist Reform in the Ancient Chinese
         State of Qin," *Challenges of the Knowledge 65 Society* 12 (2018), 524–31,
         accessed March 22, 2021, http://lexetscientia.univnt.ro/download/623_LESIJ_
         XXV_1_2018_art.010.pdf

lxxxviii Kim Collins, "Cripping Narrative: Story Telling as Activism," *Knots: An
         Undergraduate Journal of Disability Studies* 15 (2015), 31.

lxxxix   Ibid.

xc   Liselotte Frisk and Susan J. Palmer, "The Life Story of Helge Fossmo, Former
         Pastor of Knutby Filadelfia, as Told in Prison: A Narrative Analysis Approach,"
         International Journal for the Study of New Religions 6, no. 1 (2015), 51–52.

xci   Jerome Bruner, "The Narrative Creation of Self," *The Handbook of Narrative
         and Psychotherapy*, ed. Lynne E. Angus and John McLeod (Thousand Oaks,
         CA: SAGE Publications, 2004), 4.

xcii   Bruner, "The Narrative Creation of Self," 4.

xciii   William Gamson, "Policy Discourse and the Language of the Life-World,"
         in *Eigenwilligkeit und Rationalität sozialer Prozesse*, ed. Jurgen Gerhards and
         Ronald Hitzler, (e-book) (VS Verlag für Sozialwissenschaften, Springer, 1999),
         130.

xciv   Gamson, "How Storytelling Can Be Empowering," in *Culture in Mind:
         Toward a Sociology of Culture and Cognition*, ed. by Karen Cerulo (New York:
         Routledge, 2001), 197.

xcv   William Gamson, "Policy Discourse and the Language of the Life-World," 130.

xcvi   Tursun and Dawut are well-known survivors of the "re-education" camps.
         Once released from the camps, they both fled from China to the U.S., where
         they spoke before the United Nations, the U.S. Senate, and the media,
         describing experiences of torture, human rights violations, and other atrocities
         that they bore witness to, such as the murder and rape of their cellmates. Given
         how tightly the CCP tries to control information on what is occurring in
         Xinjiang, such testimony has proven to be a crucial element in the effort to get
         various states and international organizations to acknowledge the situation in
         Xinjiang as genocide.

Bibliography

Abramson, Kara. "Gender, Uyghur Identity, and the Story of Nuzugum," *The Journal of Asian Studies* 71 no. 4 (2012): 1069–91.

Azim, Fahmida, Anthony Del Col, and Josh Adams. "How I Escaped a Chinese Internment Camp," *Insider*, December 28, 2021. https://www.insider.com/comic-i-escaped-a-chinese-internment-camp-uyghur-2021-12

Bellér-Hann, Ildikó. *Community Matters in Xinjiang 1880–1949: Towards the Historical Anthropology of the Uyghur*. Leiden, Boston, MA: Brill, 2008.

Bergeron, Anne-Sophie. "The Chinese Uyghur Genocide Explained," The Organization for World Peace, March 16, 2021. https://theowp.org/the-chinese-uyghur-genocide-explained/.

Bidou, H. "Introduction," *Gazette du bon ton*, November 1–4, 1910.

Boast, Genevieve, *Tough Bliss: Restorying Life*. Createspace Independent Publishing Platform, 2018.

Bruner, Gerome. "The Narrative Creation of Self," in *The Handbook of Narrative and Psychotherapy: Practice, Theory, and Research*, edited by Lynne E. Angus and John McLeod, 3–14. Thousand Oaks, CA: SAGE Publications, 2004.

Byler, Darren. *In the Camps: China's High-Tech Penal Colony*. New York: Random House, 2021.

Campbell, Ian W. "'Our friendly rivals': Rethinking the Great Game in Ya'qub Beg's Kashgaria, 1867–77," *Central Asian Survey* 33, no. 2 (2014): 199–214.

"Canada's Parliament Declares China's Treatment of Uighurs 'Genocide,'" BBC News, February 23, 2021. https://www.bbc.com/news/world-us-canada-56163220

Carter, Adam. "Activist Accuses Chinese Government of Meddling after McMaster Speech Disrupted," *CBC News*, February 15, 2019. https://www.cbc.ca/news/canada/hamilton/mcmaster-university-china-1.5021406

Chanisheff, Söyüngül. *The Land Drenched in Tears*. Translated by Rahima Mahmut. London: Hertfordshire Press, 2018.

"China Cuts Uighur Births with IUDs, Abortion, Sterilization." *The Associated Press News*, June 29, 2020. https://apnews.com/article/ap-top-news-international-news-weekend-reads-china-health-269b3de1af34e17c1941a514f78d764c

"Chinese Ambassador Calls Uyghurs Genocide Allegations 'Lies of the Century.'" *Global News*, March 3, 2021. https://globalnews.ca/video/7674308/chinese-ambassador-calls-uighurs-genocide-allegations-lies-of-the-century

Coletta, Amanda. "Canada's 'Two Michaels' Back Home after More than 1,000 Days Imprisoned in China as Huawei's Meng Cuts Deal with U.S.," *Washington Post*,

September 25, 2021. https://www.washingtonpost.com/world/2021/09/24/canada-two-michaels-china-huawei/

Collins, Kim. "Crippling Narrative: Story Telling as Activism," *Knots: An Undergraduate Journal of Disability Studies* 15 (2015), 313–37.

CGTN "CGTN finds Mihrigul Tursun's claims false." March 14 2019, 3.51 https://www.youtube.com/watch?v=rsQxjFCh5zU

Davis, Joseph E. "Narrative and Social Movements: The Power of Stories," in *Stories of Change: Narratives and Social Movements*, edited by Joseph E. Davis, 3–30. Albany, NY: SUNY, 2002.

DeMocker, Mary. *The Parents' Guide to Climate Revolution*. Novato, CA: New World Library, 2018.

Dillon, Michael. "Xinjiang before 1949: A Historical Outline," in *Xinjiang: China's Muslim Far Northwest*, 8–22. London: Routledge Curzon, 2004.

Dooley, Connor W. "Silencing Xinjiang: The Chinese Government's Campaign against the Uyghurs," J. D. Candidate, University of Georgia School of Law, B.A. (Southern Methodist University, 2020).

Dou, Eva and Cate Cadell. "As Crackdown Eases, China's Xinjiang Faces Long Road to Rehabilitation," *Washington Post*, September 23, 2022. https://www.stripes.com/theaters/asia_pacific/2022-09-23/crackdown-eases-chinas-xinjiang-long-road-rehabilitation-7441236.html

Dunaway, David King. "The Development of Oral History in the United States: The Evolution toward Interdisciplinary," *Revista Tempo E Argumento* 10, no. 24 (2018): 115–35.

Dwyer, Adrienne, M. *The Xinjiang Conflict: Uyghur Identity, Language Policy, and Political Discourse*. Washington, D.C.: East–West Center, 2005.

"'Eradicating Ideological Viruses': China's Campaign of Repression against Xinjiang's Muslims," *Human Rights Watch*, March 14, 2019. https://www.hrw.org/report/2018/09/09/eradicating-ideological-viruses/chinas-campaign-repression-against-xinjiangs

Everington, Keoni. "Saudis Allegedly Buy 'Halal Organs' from 'Slaughtered' Xianjiang Muslims," *Taiwan News*, January 22, 2020. https://www.taiwannews.com.tw/en/news/3862578

Fine, Gary Ala. "The Storied Group: Social Movements as 'Bundles of Narratives'," in *Stories of Change: Narratives and Social Movements*, edited by Joseph E. Davis, 229–46. Albany, NY: SUNY, 2002.

Finley, Joanne Smith. "Uyghur Women between Community and State: Islamic Revival, Coercive Secularisation, Honour and Shame," in *Community Still Matters: Uyghur Culture and Society in the Central Asian Context*, edited by Aysima Mirsultan, Eric Schluessel, and Eset Sulaiman, 188–202. Copenhagen: Nordic Institute of Asian Studies (NIAS) Press, 2022.

Finley, Joanne Smith. "Why Scholars and Activists Increasingly Fear a Uyghur Genocide in Xinjiang," *Journal of Genocide Research* 23, no. 3 (2021): 348–70. https://doi.org/10.1080/14623528.2020.1848109

Fish, Stanley Eugene. *There's No Such Thing as Free Speech, and It's a Good Thing, Too.* New York: Oxford University Press, 1994.

Frisk, Liselotte and Susan J. Palmer. "The Life Story of Helge Fossmo, Former Pastor of Knutby Filadelfia, as Told in Prison: A Narrative Analysis Approach," *International Journal for the Study of New Religions* 6, no. 1 (2015): 51–73.

Gamson, William A. "How Storytelling Can Be Empowering," in *Culture in Mind: Toward a Sociology of Culture and Cognition*, edited by Karen Cerulo, 187–99. New York: Routledge, 2001.

Gamson, William A. "Policy Discourse and the Language of the Life-World," in *Eigenwilligkeit und Rationalität sozialer Prozesse*, edited by Jurgen Gerhards and Ronald Hitzler, 127–144 (e-book). VS Verlag für Sozialwissenschaften, Springer, 1999.

Gardner, Bovingdon. *The Uyghurs: Strangers in Their Own Land*. New York: Columbia University, 2010.

Gergen, Kenneth J. and Mary M. Gergen. "Narrative and the Self as Relationship," in *Advances in Experimental Social Psychology, Volume Twenty-One*, edited by Leonard Berkowitz, 17–56. San Diego, CA: Academic Press, 1988.

Gerin, Roseanne. "Belgium, Czech Republic Legislatures Pass Uyghur Genocide Declarations," *Radio Free Asia*, January 15, 2021. https://www.rfa.org/english/news/uyghur/genocide-declarations-06152021171101.html.

Greitens, Sheena Chestnut, Myunghee Lee, and Emir Yazici. "Counterterrorism and Preventive Repression: China's Changing Strategy in Xinjiang," *International Security* 44, no. 3 (2020): 9–47. https://doi.org/10.1162/isec_a_00368

Grose, Timothy. "Beautifying Uyghur Bodies: Fashion, 'Modernity,' and State Discipline in the Tarim Basin," *Monde chinois*, 63, (2020): 12–29. https://doiorg.proxy3.library.mcgill.ca/10.3917/mochi.063.0012

Grose, Timothy. "Chinese Social Media Sources Leave No Room for Denial," *HAU: Journal of Ethnographic Theory* 12 no. 2 (2022): 392–404. https://doi.org/10.1086/721745

Grose, Timothy. *Negotiating Inseparability in China: The Xinjiang Class and the Dynamics of Uyghur Identity*. Hong Kong: Hong Kong University Press, 2019.

Guttman, Ethan. *The Slaughter: Mass Killings, Organ Harvesting, and China's Secret Solution to Its Dissident Problem*. New York: Prometheus Books, 2014.

Harris, Rachel. "The New Battleground: Song-and-dance in China's Muslim Borderlands," *The World of Music* 6, no. 2 (2017): 35–55, https://www.jstor.org/stable/44841945

Harris, Rachel. *Soundscapes of Uyghur Islam*. Bloomington, IN: Indiana University Press, 2020.

Harris, Rachel. Guangtian Ha, and Maria Jaschok (eds.). *Ethnographies of Islam in China*. Honolulu, HI: University of Hawaii Press, 2020.

Hartman, Leigh. "Japanese Manga Comic Tells Story of Uyghur Oppression," *Share America*, December 26, 2019. https://share.america.gov/japanese-manga-comic-tells-story-of-uyghur-oppression/

Hideto, Sakai. "With Uighur Comic, Japanese Manga Artist Aims to Highlight Everyday 'Suffering," Reuters, December 27, 2019. https://www.reuters.com/article/us-japan-uighur-comic-idUKKBN1YV0QC

Hill, Matthew, David Campanale, and Joel Gunter. "'Their Goal Is to Destroy Everyone': Uighur Camp Detainees Allege Systematic Rape," BBC News, February 2, 2021, sec. China. https://www.bbc.com/news/world-asia-china-55794071.

Holder, Ross. "On the Interrelatedness of Human Rights, Culture and Religion: Considering the Significance of Cultural Rights in Protecting the Religious Identity of China's Uyghur Minority," *The International Journal of Human Rights*, 2020. https://doi.org/10.1080/13642987.2020.1725487

Huang, Cindy Yung-Leh. "Muslim Women at a Crossroads: Gender and Development in the Xinjiang Uyghur Autonomous Region, China." Ph.D. dissertation. University of California, Berkeley, 2009.

Janesick, J. Valerie. "Oral History as a Social Justice Project: Issues for the Qualitative Researcher," *The Qualitative Report* 12, no. 1 (2007): 111–21. https://doi.org/10.46743/2160-3715/2007.1648

Janesick, J. Valerie. "Oral History Interviewing: Issues and Possibilities," in *The Oxford Handbook of Qualitative Research*, edited by Patricia Leavy, 300–14. Oxford: Oxford University Press, 2014.

Kadeer, Rebiya and Alexandra Cavelius. *Dragon Fighter: One Woman's Epic Struggle or Peace with China*. San Diego, CA: Kales Press, 2009.

Kenneth, Suddaby and Landau Judith. "Positive and Negative Timelines: A Technique for Restorying," *Family Process* 37, no. 3 (1998): 287–98.

Kleinig, John. "Whistleblower" in *The Encyclopedia of Governance*, edited by Mark Brevil. New York: SAGE, 2006.

Kvale, Steinar, *Doing Interviews*. Sage Qualitative Research Kit, 63–5. London: SAGE Publications, 2007.

Lieblich, Amia, Rivka Tuval-Maschiach, and Tammar Zilber. *Narrative Research: Reading, Analysis and Interpretation*. Thousand Oaks, CA: SAGE, 1998.

Leibold, James and Timothy Grose. "Islamic Veiling in Xinjiang: The Political and Societal Struggle to Define Uyghur Female Adornment," *The China Journal* 76 (2016): 78–102. https://www.journals.uchicago.edu/doi/pdf/10.1086/683283

Leonard, Barbara. "Netherlands Lashes out against 'Genocide' of Uyghur People in China," *Courthouse News Service*, February 25, 2021. https://www.courthousenews.com/netherlands-lashes-out-against-genocide-of-uighur-people-in-china/

MacLeod, Chris. "Huseyin Celil Is the Forgotten Canadian Detained in China," 2021. *Toronto Star*, March 15, 2021. https://www.thestar.com/opinion/contributors/2021/03/15/huseyin-celil-is-the-forgotten-canadian-detained-in-china.html

Mahmood, Saba. *Politics of Piety: The Islamic Revival and the Feminist Subject*. Princeton, NJ: Princeton University Press, 2012.

Mahmut, Dilmurat and Joanne Smith Finley. "'A Man Works on the Land, a Woman Works for Her Man': Building on Jarring's Fascination with Eastern Turki Proverbs," in *Kashgar Revisited: Commemorating the 10th Anniversary of the Death of Ambassador Gunnar Jarring,* edited by Ildicó. Bellér-Hann, B. Schlyter, and Jun Sugawara, 302–30. Leiden, Boston, MA: Brill, 2017.

Mahmut, Rahima. "Interpreting Witness Statements from the Uyghur Genocide," *Society and Space,* December 7, 2020. www.societyandspace.org. https://www.societyandspace.org/articles/interpreting-witness-statements-from-the-uyghur-genocide

Mahmut, Rahima. "Opinion: With Trump Going, Who in the Free World Will Stand up for Uighurs Now?," *The Independent,* November 30, 2020. https://www.independent.co.uk/voices/trump-china-uighur-oppression-human-rights-b1763945.html

Matas, David and David Kilgour. *Bloody Harvest: Organ Harvesting of Falun Gong Practitioners in China.* Woodstock, ON: Seraphim Editions, 2009.

McAdams, Dan P. and Philip J. Bowman. "Narrating Life's Turning Points: Redemption and Contamination," in *Turns in the Road: Narrative Studies of Lives in Transition,* edited by Dan P. McAdams, Ruthellen Josselson, and Amia Lieblich, 3–34. Washington, D.C.: American Psychological Association, 2001.

Millward, James. "China's Fruitless Repression of the Uighurs," *The New York Times,* September 28, 2014. https://www.nytimes.com/2014/09/29/opinion/chinas-fruitless-repression-of-the-uighurs.html

Millward, James. "Violent Separatism in Xinjiang: A Critical Assessment," *Policy Studies* 6. Washington, D.C.: East-West Center, 2004. https://www.eastwestcenter.org/system/tdf/private/PS006.pdf?file=1&type=node&id=32006

Millward, James, and Dahlia Peterson. "China's System of Oppression in Xinjiang: How It Developed and How to Curb It," *Brookings,* September 14, 2020. https://www.brookings.edu/research/chinas-system-of-oppression-in-xinjiang-how-it-developed-and-how-to-curb-it/

Mlynář, Jakub, and Jamie Lewis. *Analysing Oral Histories: Social Roles and Narrative Self-Regulation in Holocaust Survivors' Testimonies.* London: SAGE Publications, 2017. https://doi.org/10.4135/9781473999152 (accessed November 16th 2023).

Moses, Dirk A. "Paranoia and Partisanship: Genocide Studies, Holocaust Historiography, and the 'Apolitical Conjuncture,'" *The Historical Journal* 54, no. 2 (2011): 553–83.

Newline Institute for Strategy and Policy. "The Uyghur Genocide: An Examination of China's Breach of the 1948 Genocide Convention," March 2021. https://newlinesinstitute.org/wp-content/uploads/Chinas-Breaches-of-the-GC3-2.pdf

Niewenhuis, Lucas. "China's 'Social Re-Engineering' of Uyghurs, Explained by Darren Byler," *SupChina,* August 15, 2019. https://signal.supchina.com/chinas-social-re-engineering-of-uyghurs-explained-by-darren-byler/

Nomura, Hataru. "Proof of China's Organ Harvesting Found in Xinjiang," *The Libertyweb Global,* September 21, 2018. https://eng.the-liberty.com/2018/7286/

"Once Oppressed, Xinjiang's Uyghur Women Take on Chinese Government," *ANI News,* March 14, 2021. https://www.aninews.in/news/world/asia/once-oppressed-xinjiangs-uyghur-women-take-on-chinese-government20210314092314/ (accessed November 16th 2023).

Palmer, Susan J. and Abdulmuqtedir Udun. "Beijing Olympics – Where Are the Uyghur Athletes?," *Ottawa Citizen*, February 16, 2022. https://ottawacitizen.com/opinion/palmer-and-udun-beijing-olympics-where-are-the-uyghur-athletes

Palmer, Susan J., Marie-Ève Melanson, Dilmurat Mahmut, and Abdulmuqtedir Udun. "The Uyghurs in the Diaspora in Canada," 2021 Survey Report, vol. 3 no. 1 (2021): The Uyghurs in Diaspora August 29, 2022: 1–12. https://creor-ejournal.library.mcgill.ca

Pamuk, Humeyra. "Pompeo Says U.S. Troubled by Reports of China Harassing Families of Uighur Activists," Reuters, November 5, 2019. https://www.reuters.com/article/us-usa-china-muslims-pompeo-idUSKBN1XF20S

"Photo Report on the Hungarotex Export Fashion Show," *This Is Fashion*, June 4, 1966.

Ramzy, Austin and Chris Buckley. "'Absolutely No Mercy': Leaked Files Expose How China Organized Mass Detentions of Muslims," *The New York Times*, November 16, 2019. https://www.nytimes.com/interactive/2019/11/16/world/asia/china-xinjiang-documents.html

Robins, Robert S. and Jerrod M. Post. *Political Paranoia: The Psychopolitics of Hatred*. New Haven, CT: Yale University Press, 1997.

Roberts, S. R. *The War on the Uyghurs: China's Internal Campaign against a Muslim Minority*. Princeton, NJ: Princeton University Press, 2020.

Robins, Robert S. and Jerrod M. Pos. *Political Paranoia: The Psychopolitics of Hatred*. New Haven, CT: Yale University Press, 1997.

Ruether, Rosemary Radford. *Sexism and God Talk: Towards a Feminist Theology*. Boston, MA: Beacon Press, 1993.

Ruth, Ingram. "Where Is Uyghur Folklore Expert Rahile Dawut?," *The Diplomat*, November 23, 2020. https://thediplomat.com/2020/11/where-is-uyghur-folklore-expert-rahile-dawut/

Ruser, Nathan. "There Is Now More Evidence than Ever that China Is Imprisoning Uighurs," *The Guardian*, September 24, 2020. https://www.theguardian.com/commentisfree/2020/sep/24/china-imprisoning-uighurs-satellite-images-xinjiang

Samuel, Sigal. "Internet Sleuths are Hunting for China's Secret Internment Camps for Muslims," *The Atlantic*, September 15, 2018. https://www.theatlantic.com/international/archive/2018/09/china-internment-camps-muslim-uighurs-satellite/569878/

Seymour, James D. "Xinjiang's Production and Construction Corps, and the Sinification of Eastern Turkestan," *Inner Asia* 2, no. 2 (2000): 171–93. http://www.jstor.org/stable/23615556

Schein, Louisa. "Gender and Internal Orientalism in China," *Modern China*, 23, no. 1 (1997): 69–98. https://doi.org/10.1177/009770049702300103

Shamseden, Zubayra. "I Have Revised My Idea of What a Uighur Heroine Should Be," *China File*, 2019, April 19. https://www.chinafile.com/reporting-opinion/viewpoint/i-have-revised-my-idea-of-what-uighur-heroine-should-be

Shih, Gerry and Dake Kang. "Muslims Forced to Drink Alcohol and Eat Pork in China's 'Re-Education' Camps, Former Inmate Claims," *The Independent*, May 18, 2018.

https://www.independent.co.uk/news/world/asia/china-re-education-muslims-ramadan-xinjiang-eat-pork-alcohol-communist-xi-jinping-a8357966.html

Smith, Richard Cándida. "Storytelling as Experience" (Review Essay), *The Oral History Review* 22, no. 2 (Winter 1995): 87–90.

Smith Finley, Joanne. *The Art of Symbolic Resistance: Uyghur Identities and Uyghur–Han Relations in Contemporary Xinjiang*. Leiden: Brill, 2013.

Smith Finley, Joanne. "Education, Religion and Identity among Uyghur Hostesses in Ürümchi," in *Language, Education and Uyghur Identity in Urban Xinjiang*, edited by Joanne Smith Finley and Zang Xiaowei, 176–93. London: Routledge, 2015.

Smith Finley, Joanne. "'Ethnic Anomaly' or Modern Uyghur Survivor? A Case Study of the Minkaohan Hybrid Identity in Xinjiang," in *Situating the Uyghurs between China and Central Asia*, edited by Ildikó Bellér-Hann, Joanne Smith Finley, and M. Cristina Cesàro, 219–37. Aldershot: Ashgate, 2007.

Sohail, Sabrina. "CFU Condemns 'Spokesperson of the People's Government of XUAR's' Response to the Xinjiang Police Files," *Campaign for Uyghurs*, January 5, 2023. https://campaignforuyghurs.org/cfu-condemns-spokesperson-of-the-peoples-government-of-xuars-response-to-the-xinjiang-police-files

Spengemann, Sven and Fonseca, Peter. "*The Human Rights Situation of Uyghurs in Xinjiang, China: Report of the Standing Committee on Foreign Affairs and International Development Subcommittee on International Human Rights*," House of Commons Canada, March 2021. https://www.ourcommons.ca/Content/Committee/432/FAAE/Reports/RP11164859/sdirrp04/sdirrp04-e.pdf

"'Thank the Party!': China Tries to Brainwash Muslims in Camps," *CBC News*, May 17, 2018. https://www.cbc.ca/news/world/china-internment-camps-1.4666686

Tobin, David. *Securing Chinas Northwest Frontier: Identity and Insecurity in Xinjiang*. Cambridge: Cambridge University Press, 2020.

Tohti, Ilham. "Present-Day Ethnic Problems in Xinjiang Uighur Autonomous Region: Overview and Recommendations (1) – Unemployment," translated by Cindy Carter, *China Change*, April 22, 2015. http://chinachange.org/2015/04/22/present-day-ethnic-problems-in-xinjiang-uighur-autonomous-region-overview-and-recommendations-1/

Turdush, Rukiye. "Why Canada Should Take the Lead in Recognizing China's Crimes against Uyghurs as Genocide," *Medium*, September 23, 2020. https://medium.com/@rukiyeturdush/why-canada-should-take-the-lead-in-recognizing-chinas-crimes-against-uyghurs-as-genocide-df11d386e5bd

"US Voices Disgust at China Boast of Uighur Population Control." *Arab News*, January 9, 2021. https://www.arabnews.com/node/1789511/world

Turdush, Rukiye and Magnus Fiskesjö. "Dossier: Uyghur Women in China's Genocide," *Genocide Studies and Prevention: An International Journal*, 15, no. 1 (2021): 22–43. https://doi.org/10.5038/1911-9933.15.1.1834

Turkel, Nury. *No Escape: The True Story of China's Genocide of the Uyghurs*. New York: Hanover Square Press, 2022.

Tynen, Sarah. "Belonging between Inclusion and Exclusion: Dimensions of Ethno-Cultural Identity for Uyghur Women in Xinjiang, China," *Geopolitics* 26, no. 4 (2019): 1243–66. https://doi.org/10.1080/14650045.2019.1686360

"UHRP Welcomes Taiwan's Resolution on Atrocities against Uyghurs," *Uyghur Human Rights Project*, January 3, 2023. https://uhrp.org/statement/uhrp-welcomes-taiwans-resolution-on-atrocities-against-uyghurs/

VanderKlippe, Nathan. "China Detaining Hundreds of Thousands of Uyghurs in Prison-like Centres: Report," *The Globe and Mail*, May 15, 2018. https://www.theglobeandmail.com/world/article-china-detaining-hundreds-of-thousands-of-uyghurs-in-prison-like/

Wines, Michael. "To Protect an Ancient City, China Moves to Raze It," *The New York Times*, May 27, 2009. https://www.nytimes.com/2009/05/28/world/asia/28kashgar.html

Withnall, Adam. "China is Killing Religious and Ethnic Minorities and Harvesting their Organs, UN Human Rights Council Told," *Independent*, September 24, 2019. https://www.independent.co.uk/news/world/asia/china-religious-ethnic-minorities-uighur-muslim-harvest-organs-un-human-rights-a9117911.html

Wong, Edward, and Chris Buckley. "U.S. Says China's Repression of Uighurs Is 'Genocide,'" *The New York Times*, January 19, 2021. https://www.nytimes.com/2021/01/19/us/politics/trump-china-xinjiang.html.

Wood, Bryan. "What Is Happening with the Uighurs in China?," *PBS NewsHour*, October 7, 2019. https://www.pbs.org/newshour/features/uighurs/

Xin, Liu and Fan Lingzhi. "Relatives of So-called Uyghur Activists Slam Pompeo's Detention Claim," *Global Times*, November 17, 2019. https://www.globaltimes.cn/page/201911/1170249.shtml

Xinhua. "White Paper: Xinjiang Inseparable Part of China," July 21, 2019, *China Daily Hong Kong*. https://www.chinadailyhk.com/articles/228/219/155/1563683130475.html#:~:text=Xinjiang%20has%20long%20been%20an

Yu, Cindy. "Have Xinjiang's Camps Been Closed?," February 6, 2023, *The Spectator*. https://www.spectator.co.uk/podcast/have-xinjiangs-camps-been-closed/

Yuchun, Lian, Li Yuanbin, and Li Dabiao. "Xinjiang Think Tank Unveils Adrian Zenz as Swindler under Academic Disguise," *Global Times*, August 9, 2020. https://www.globaltimes.cn/content/1197187.shtml

Zang, Xiaowei. "Uyghur–Han Earnings Differentials in Ürümchi," *The China Journal*, 65 (2011): 141–55.

Zenz, Adrian, "Break Their Lineage, Break Their Roots,'" *Human Rights Watch*, April 19, 2021. https://www.hrw.org/report/2021/04/19/break-their-lineage-break-their-roots/chinas-crimes-against-humanity-targeting

Zenz, Adrian. "China's Own Documents Show Potentially Genocidal Sterilization Plans in Xinjiang," *Foreign Policy*, July 1, 2020. https://foreignpolicy.com/2020/07/01/china-documents-uighur-genocidal-sterilization-xinjiang/

Zenz, Adrian. "The Karakax List: Dissecting the Anatomy of Beijing's Internment Drive in Xinjiang," *Journal of Political Risk* 8, no. 2 (2020, February). https://www.jpolrisk.com/karakax/

Zenz, Adrian. "Sterilizations, IUDs, and Mandatory Birth Control: The CCP's Campaign to Suppress Uyghur Birthrates in Xinjiang," *Victims of Communism*, June 29, 2020. https://victimsofcommunism.org/publication/sterilizations-iuds-and-mandatory-birth-control-the-ccps-campaign-to-suppress-uyghur-birthrates-in-xinjiang/

Zenz, Adrian. "The Xinjiang Police Files: Re-Education Camp Security and Political Paranoia in the Xinjiang Uyghur Autonomous Region," *The Journal of the European Association for Chinese Studies* 3 (2022, December): 263–311. https://doi.org/10.25365/jeacs.2022.3.zenz (accessed November 16th 2023).

Index